P9-DGE-158

SALAD PEOPLE

To my mother, Betty Katzen, with love, appreciation, and admiration

Acknowledgments

Nicole Geiger, my editor at Tricycle Press, has provided invaluable support to my children's cookbook projects since their inception over a decade ago. Her passion and focus have been a blessing for which I feel very fortunate.

Bushels of appreciation also go out to Summer Laurie, Rebecca Pepper, and Jasmine Star, editorial team; as well as to Laura Mancuso, publicist; Nancy Austin and Mona Meisami, design team; and Mary Ann Anderson, Tricycle Press production wizard.

Thanks to Ann Henderson, my *Pretend Soup* coauthor and early educator of my children, for her inspiration and example.

Zachary, Maya, and Tessa Bond—and their parents, David and Jenny—are currently the little people in my life; their enthusiasm for food in all its manifestations has resparked my own.

Jenny Wheeler-Stein and Eve Shames provided much-appreciated classroom and kitchen backup and recipe testing. Thanks so much to both of you for your calm and cheerful presence!

The teachers and students at Step One Nursery School in Berkeley, California, have been wonderful cooking partners! Many thanks to all of you for welcoming me into your magical space and allowing me to cook with you.

Finally, I'd like to thank the teachers from Mills College Children's School, Oakland, California—Christine Kaes, Heather Grey, and Anna Elbers—for their expertise and support.

Contents

I don't like the spicy sauce because I'm only four and a quarter. Maybe when I'm older. —NATE

I'm going to be four, too. (When?) In a minute. —RAYMOND

Children love to cook, and even those as young as three or four are drawn to the kitchen with a tremendous sense of curiosity and respect. I learned a great deal about this over a decade ago from my children's preschool teacher, Ann Henderson. Cooking was a significant and regular event in her classroom, and to me, at the time, this was downright revelatory! I had not cooked with my own kids at home, beyond letting them "help" with stirring or buttering bread, or perhaps just setting the table. But when I witnessed my son's enthusiasm—both "in action" in the preschool kid-sized kitchen area and also in his exuberant reports on the results—I realized I had overlooked an important possibility. I had underestimated the willingness of small children to approach cooking with an open mind and with the goodwill to effect something real.

Greatly inspired by Ann's classroom cooking projects, I invited her to work with me on a cookbook for very small children to use at home with their parents. That collaboration became *Pretend Soup and Other Real Recipes: A Cookbook for Preschoolers and Up*, which, as of this writing, is going into its twelfth printing and approaching 200,000 copies sold! So you might wonder, "Why a sequel? What will *Salad People* provide that I can't find in *Pretend Soup*?" The answer is simple: As I have continued cooking with little kids over the past decade, our repertoire has greatly expanded. And this all-new crop of preschooler-friendly recipes is the happy result.

The enduring popularity of *Pretend Soup* illustrates the tremendous potential for a meaningful relationship between young children and cooking. A growing number of families around the country can attest to the enthusiasm with which young children will embrace healthy foods, like fruit, vegetables, soups, and salads, without needing to be lured by sugar, frosting, or gumdrops. Pure, good food carries its own appeal, an appeal that is enhanced many times over by the opportunity for an up-close, hands-on experience that makes it happen. Within these preschool-tested cooking projects, small miracles can take place, and a lifelong appreciation of food can begin at an earlier age than any of us might once have thought possible. I can't encourage you enough to invite your own youngster into the kitchen in a serious (and fun) way to find this out for yourselves!

On a personal note: This book is named for a lunch dish that my mother used to make for me and my brothers on special occasions. We called it Faces, and it was a cheerful montage of cheese, fruit, and vegetables arranged to look like little people, one per plate. I remember vividly how impressed I was by this creative, evocative dish. Looking back, I now realize that it sparked my first realization of the visual and emotional power of colorful, fresh, lovingly prepared food. Decades later, my new-fangled version of Faces is a dish renamed Salad People by my preschooler friends, and it opens this new collection of children's recipes. I hope these ideas will launch you and the youngsters you love into a new chapter of joyful kitchen adventures and food appreciation!

Mollie Katzen

Berkeley, California
August 2005

Salad People: An Owner's Manual

Salad People is set up exactly as its predecessor, *Pretend Soup*. If you are acquainted with that book, the following descriptions and explanations will be familiar.

The twenty recipes presented here were tested both at home and in a preschool setting, with children ranging in age from just under three to six years old. How did I decide which recipes to include? Of all the recipes we attempted, these are the ones I found to be most accessible and interesting to this age group. There were many variables, including (but not limited to) the children's desire to eat the end product. I also took into account attention span, variety of ingredients and tasks, color, temperature, texture, and flavor. I wanted to include as many healthy recipes (without broadcasting them as such) as I could get away with, and to minimize, if not entirely eliminate, sweets and desserts.

I found that a terrific way to draw children to good food is to have them make salads and soups, for which kids have a surprising degree of enthusiasm. Another effective approach is the make-your-own concept, where an assortment of attractive fruits and vegetables are placed within reach (as in a salad bar) and the children get to customize their own portions (such as Polka Dot Rice, Tiny Tacos, Salad People, and Green Garden Dip). Older children—and even many parents—also showed interest in these recipes, which is why the title of this book suggests "For Preschoolers and Up," rather than indicating a ceiling on the age range. But above all, I have found that what most effectively attracts kids to healthy food is the opportunity to prepare it with their own hands. Pride of accomplishment is key! "I like it because I made it myself" is the refrain I hear most often from proud little chefs, who are beyond pleased to be invited into this adult realm.

You will notice that each recipe gets a double treatment—a full four pages. The first two pages are for the adult helper, including detailed setup instructions and a conventional recipe format. Next comes a pictorial version, designed specifically for very young cooks (even prereaders!) to follow. Before you begin, read through the adult section of the recipe and get everything—right down to the last spoon—ready and in place. This will minimize interruptions once you start, allowing everyone involved to concentrate fully and safely on the project.

If your child is only three or four years old, you will probably want to do most of the food preparation and setup ahead of time. But there are a few preliminary tasks in each recipe that kids might want to "help" with, especially if they are older. I have indicated those jobs in the recipe notes. If you are working with several children of various ages, you can always assign simpler activities, like washing vegetables or arranging small bowls, to the younger ones.

I recommend that your child use regular adult-sized utensils, rather than gimmicky made-for-children ones. I find that a long-handled wooden spoon is the most effective mixing tool, and that a small whisk (they come in umpteen sizes) is the best way for a child to beat an egg. Often, a very simple gadget that an adult might take for granted can be tremendously exciting to a child. (For example, a plain set of measuring spoons and cups can be a wonderful—and much appreciated—birthday gift for a five-year-old.) Also, I have found that the quality of utensils makes a huge difference. A well-made handheld kitchen gadget with a child-friendly grip can make it possible for a young chef to perform tasks that utensils of lesser design might inhibit.

When cooking with children, always use larger containers than you think necessary, so that there is plenty of elbow room and an insurance policy against spills. A one-size-too-big liquid measuring cup and a several-sizes-larger-than-you'd-think mixing bowl, regardless of the volume of food being handled, can make all the difference in the child's confidence.

Don't worry about spills—or lumps or eggshells in the batter. Just cheerfully correct the situation and move along, as this is all part of the normal cooking experience. A child who feels secure about messes will also feel free to keep trying. That said, there are certain steps you can take to avoid excessive "inadvertent kitchen redecoration." The adult pages of each recipe will walk you through the specifics. Beyond this, just keep plenty of damp paper towels handy—and keep on smiling.

Adults tend to see cooking as primarily goal-oriented (dinner on the table), but for small children, the main event is the process itself. We all know that children can be picky eaters. It's possible that your young chef may walk away from the project once it is finished without wanting to sample the result. Younger children might be more focused on feeding the dish to you or to a favorite stuffed animal. Other times, a child will eat with abandon, requesting seconds and thirds. Try to stay neutral about the eating part, even though you may be understandably concerned about waste. We can help children develop a healthy relationship with food by encouraging them to discover what they don't like to eat as well as what they do.

Although some of these recipes are substantial enough to become a hearty snack or even lunch, I recommend scheduling the cooking session for in-between times, when you and your child are relaxed and in the mood for a shared experience—and not particularly hungry. That way, goal orientation, frustration, and tension can be avoided, and pleasure can prevail. The true prize upon which to focus is pure enjoyment—of the tasks and of one another. If you happen to get a meal out of the ritual, consider it a bonus! My hope is that every aspect of cooking with your child will be delightful for all involved and that your child's interest in cooking and eating will continue throughout the years.

What Do Children Gain from Cooking?

- A blossoming of creativity and a sense of aesthetics
- Confidence and self-esteem; a feeling of accomplishment
- Preliminary math skills (measuring, counting, sequencing of events)
- Prereading and beginning reading skills (numeral, symbol, and word recognition; left-to-right cueing)
- Science awareness (enhanced powers of observation; increased understanding of time and of cause and effect, chemistry, and temperature)
- Small motor skills; hand-eye coordination
- Strength and endurance (stirring a thick batter or squeezing a lemon by hand can be hard work if you are only 3 feet tall!)
- Patience and self-control (waiting for those Chewy Energy Circles to come out of the oven is a challenge!)
- Language skills (observing, describing, predicting)
- Ability to follow directions
- A sense of teamwork

- A greater "community" sense of connection to the household or classroom
- Food literacy (an openness to trying new foods, familiarity with healthy foods and where they come from, understanding the interrelationship of ingredients)
- A lifelong awareness and appreciation of cooking and good eating that will bring great health and other rich rewards!

Safety Tips

- Never leave a child alone when cooking together. Please emphasize to young children that, although they are now doing cooking projects with you or another adult, they are not to attempt to cook alone or unsupervised.
- Try to do everything at a level that enables a small child to see and reach as needed. Ideally you will be working at a child-sized table, using a tabletop electric skillet for any child-centered cooking. That way, you can sit with your children and work side by side, rather than dealing with kids on high stools in front of a stove.
- Keep machines (including toasters) unplugged when not in use.
- Everyone (adults included) should wash hands before starting.
- Thorough setup is key to the safety, success, and enjoyment of all involved. The more complete the setup, the better able you and your children will be to focus, uninterrupted, on the project.
- Everyone involved should wear short sleeves, or long sleeves firmly rolled up and out of the way.
- Discuss safety in simple, clear terms, especially when a task could be dangerous. Example: "We are turning on the heat now. The pan will get very hot, and could burn you if you touch it." Younger children will need frequent reminders, but try to keep the tone upbeat so children will respect the safety challenges of the kitchen without becoming fearful.
- If you are using a regular gas stove, turn off the flame before you and your young chefs stir, turn, or flip the food. Then turn it back on again when you are finished. If your stove is electric, be sure to warn children that it will stay hot even after it has been turned off. I recommend making one or two small "HOT!" signs and placing them in freestanding holders in front of or near a hot pot on the stove.
- Keep the handles of hot pots and pans pointed toward the back of the work area and away from the edge.
- Have an easily accessible fire extinguisher in the kitchen, and know how to use it. To put out smaller fires, use salt or baking soda, not water. If anyone's clothing should catch fire, the rule is "Stop, drop, and roll!" (Children should know this for fire safety in general.)
- All interactions with hot ovens and sharp knives are for adults only! No exceptions!
- Children can help put food into blenders and food processors, and can push the buttons. Adults should do everything that involves contact with the blades.
- The only cutting tools appropriate for small children are regular serrated dinner knives, strong plastic picnic knives, vegetable peelers, scissors, egg slicers, and standing graters with large holes. All of these items require adult supervision, especially the grater. Teach children that cutting with a knife is a back-and-forth motion—otherwise they will tend to just push down. For younger children, you can put a piece of colored tape on the knife handle, so they will remember which end to hold. "Hand stays on the tape" is the mantra here.
- Once warm soup is served, kids should stay put and eat in place, rather than walking to another location with a full bowl.

Kids' Own Rules

No walking away with knives! —*Theo*

Be careful when it's in the oven. Stay still! —*Melia*

When the food is hot we can look with our eyes, but not with our hands. —*Leah*

Say "No thank you" instead of "I hate that!" —*Sarah*

Stir slowly because we don't want to get it on our clothes.
We don't want to get it on our shoes, either. —*Sarah Jane*

The "hot" signs don't feel hot. You can touch those. —*Zachary*

Don't start cooking without a grown-up because the grown-up has to help. —*Orianna*

Don't run in the kitchen or you could bash into cabinets. —*Ethan*

Don't carry too many things until someday when you have big-enough hands. —*Julia*

My mom lets me stir the hot soup, but she says, "Be careful, Mia!" —*Mia*

I think you have to be six to like spicy food. —*Eli*

You can't stand on a stove. It's not a climbing structure. —*Molly*

Go on the other side of the kitchen when Mama takes
the hot stuff out of the oven. —*Rebecca*

Touch the oatmeal with your spoon but not with your finger. —*Tyler*

Don't put food on your arms. —*Nyko*

The Critics Rave:

We're gonna make people out of food! —JACK

I'm gonna make my sister. —THEO

Maybe I should make a carrot zipper. —SIMONE

Strawberry hair! —SERAFINA

To the Grown-ups:

Children will get deeply involved with this concept, which is all about creating a miniature person out of cheese, fruit, vegetables, and perhaps even pasta. In addition to being a cross between an art project and a great snack or lunch, this recipe presents a wonderful opportunity to introduce new foods—or at least new food combinations—to young children.

There is no right or wrong way to make a Salad Person. In fact, if your child doesn't feel like making something representational, it's fine to make a food design instead. In either case, let your youngster guide the experience as inspiration occurs.

Cooking Hints and Safety Tips (please review pages 11–15):

- ✦ Children can help with some of the preparations, such as slicing strawberries and bananas, grating carrots, or spreading peanut butter into celery. They also enjoy helping place all the various components in small bowls and setting everything up.
- ✦ The Salad Person's face can be made with cottage cheese or yogurt. Children of color might prefer to use coffee or chocolate yogurt so the Salad Person can look like family.
- ✦ You can firm up any flavor of yogurt by placing it in a paper-lined cone coffee filter over a bowl for a few hours—or even overnight. The whey will drip out of the yogurt, leaving behind a firmer curd, often referred to as "yogurt cheese." Keep in mind that you'll end up with only about 60 percent of the original volume.
- ✦ The amounts are quite flexible, so just estimate the quantities.

Children's Tools: Cutting boards and child-appropriate knives (if the children are going to help with the cutting); spoons for scooping; a plate and fork for each person

Salad People Recipe

Cored pear halves, peel optional (fresh and ripe, or canned and drained)

Cottage cheese or very firm yogurt

Strips of cheese (cut wide and thin, to be limbs)

Sliced bananas (cut into vertical spears as well as rounds)

Cantaloupe or honeydew (cut into 4-inch slices)

Celery sticks (plain or stuffed with nut butter)

Shredded carrots (in long strands, if possible)

Sliced strawberries

Raisins

Dried cranberries

Pitted cherries

Cherry tomatoes

Blueberries

Peas

Cooked angel hair pasta, or a "curly" variety

Parsley sprigs

Small spinach leaves

Sliced black olives

Sliced radishes

1) Place a pear half in the center of each plate, flat side down.
2) Arrange a round scoop of cottage cheese or very firm yogurt above the narrow top of the pear, so that the cheese or yogurt looks like a head and the pear looks like a torso.
3) Create arms and legs from strips of cheese, banana spears, melon slices, or celery sticks (stuffed or plain).
4) Create hair, facial features, hands, feet, buttons, zippers, hats, and so forth from any combination of the remaining ingredients.
5) Name it and eat!

YIELD: Flexible! Just put out a lot of food. Store the leftovers for next time, which will likely be soon.

Salad People

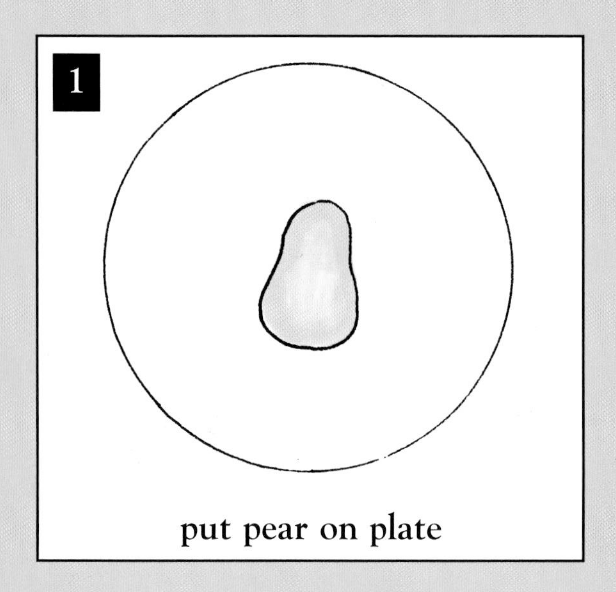

put pear on plate

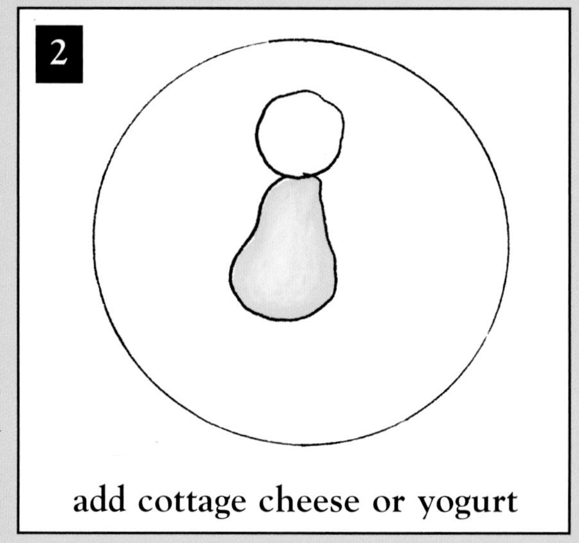

add cottage cheese or yogurt

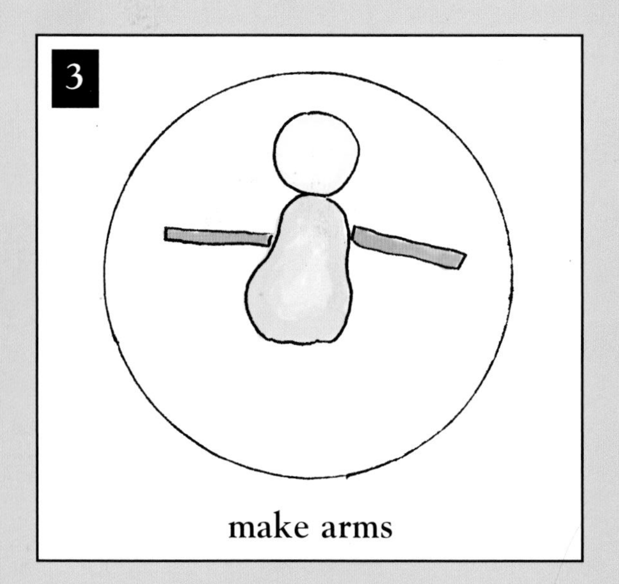

make arms

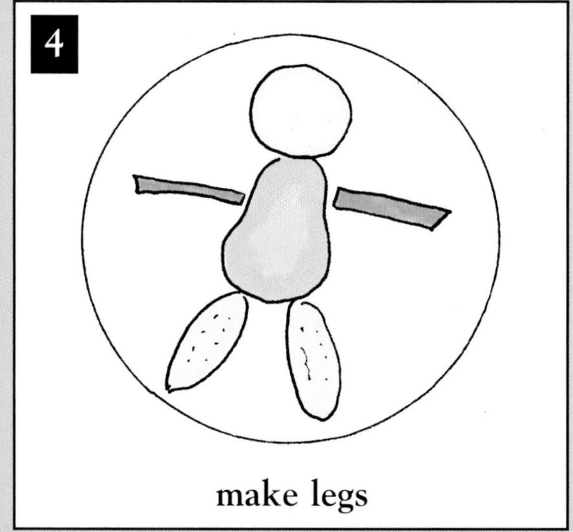

make legs

make hair

make a face

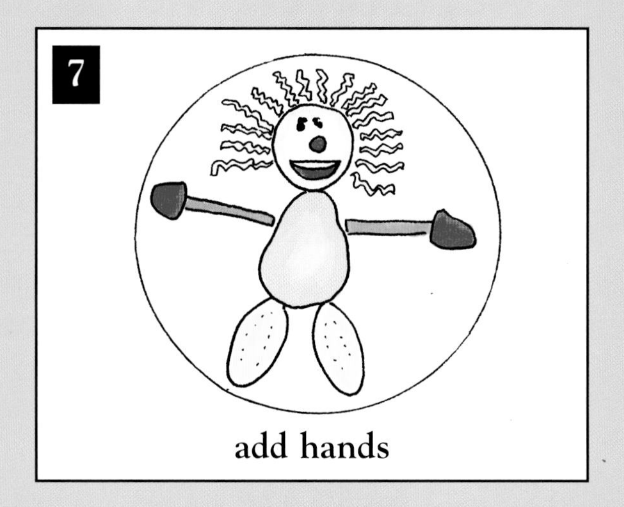

add hands

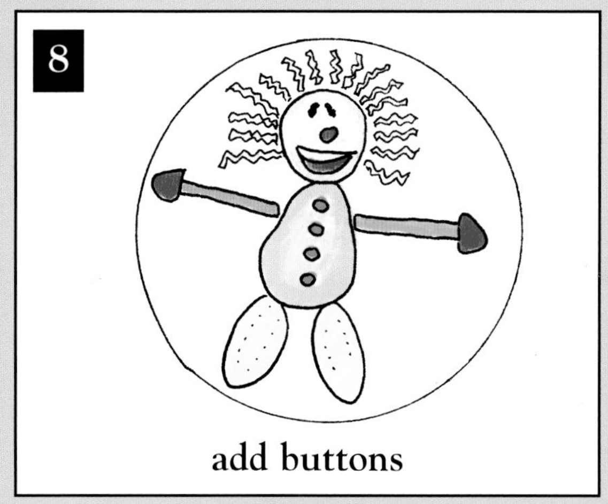

add buttons

EAT!

The Critics Rave:

Hey bean! Get off my fork! —JACK

When I leave off the top chip, it looks like a flower. —KATE

Lookit! A sandwich! —TYLER

I want to make more tacos so I can be a fast runner in my new shoes. —CHARLEY

You could eat fourteen, but then you'd have a tummy ache. —THEO

To the Grown-ups:

In this refreshing departure from burritos and quesadillas, younger children can customize their own Mexican snack in small doses, tasting the different components either separately or together in varying combinations. Kids love small-scale food, and the miniature aspect of this recipe is quite appealing to them, especially when the various toppings are set up with small spoons. (We used baby-feeding spoons for our recipe tests, and the kids just loved this!)

You can expand this project by making homemade versions of refried beans, tortilla chips, guacamole, and/or salsa. Older kids enjoy doing all the various tasks involved, and younger kids are always happy to mash anything—especially beans and avocado. So by all means, broaden the experience if you have the time and inclination. At the very least, the kids can get involved in grating the cheese.

Cooking Hints and Safety Tips (please review pages 11–15):

- Ultraclean hands today!
- The beans can be at room temperature (grated cheese can just be pressed, rather than melted, into the beans) and everything else can be cold. This way, the kids (and adults) don't have to deal with safety issues regarding heat.

- Put all the toppings in small bowls before the children begin.
- Tiny spoons (baby-feeding spoons) make this easier and more fun for small kids.
- Keep damp paper towels handy, and serve with plenty of napkins.

Children's Tools: Standing grater with large holes (if the children will be grating); a plate for each person; small spoons

Tiny Tacos Recipe

1 standard package tortilla chips (small, round, flat ones work best)
One 15-ounce can refried beans
1 cup guacamole
1 cup fresh salsa
1/3 pound jack cheese, grated

1) Lay the chips on a plate.
2) Spoon a small amount of refried beans on each chip.
3) Spoon on dabs of guacamole and salsa.
4) Sprinkle on some cheese.
5) Eat open-faced, or add chips on top to make "sandwiches."

YIELD: Enough for 6 kids to snack heartily

Tiny Tacos

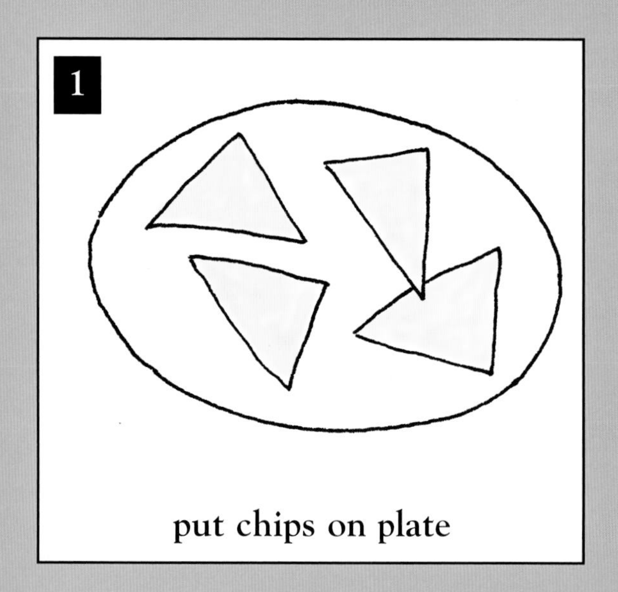

put chips on plate

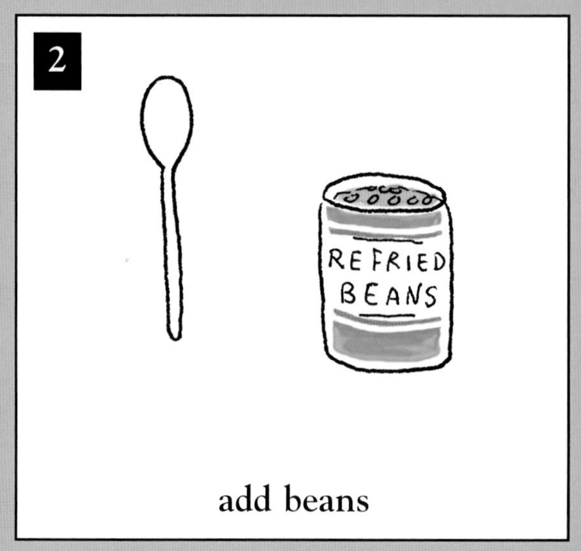

add beans

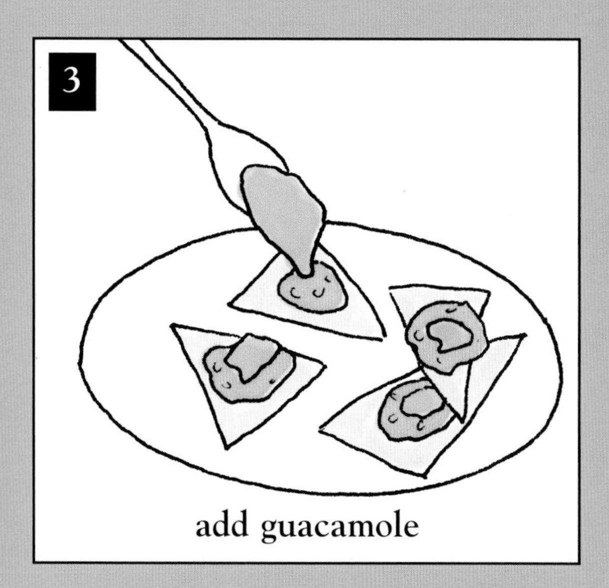

add guacamole

add salsa

sprinkle cheese

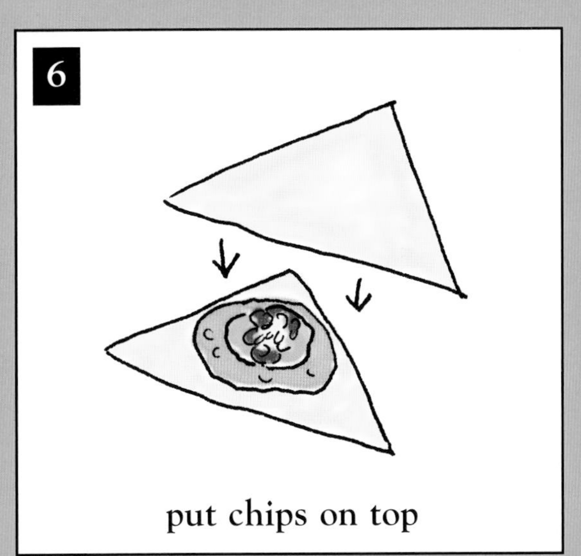

put chips on top

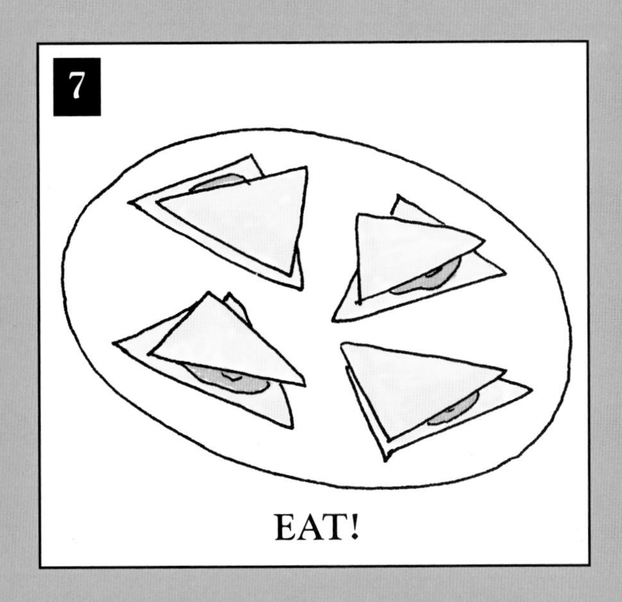

EAT!

The Critics Rave:

I ate some of this last morning. —ZACHARY

These were oats before we made them into a different stuff. —GABRIELLE

I'm eating the cranberries because they're good. —NATE

To the Grown-ups:

Get out the biggest bowl you can find and have your children roll up their sleeves and dig in! For an extra creative opportunity, let the children choose from a variety of dried fruit. And when you serve this the traditional way, in a bowl with milk, the kids may want to drink the milk afterward. It will taste like butterscotch.

You'll need to tailor this recipe if any of the kids have nut allergies, or if you are concerned about small particles, like sunflower seeds. You can substitute additional rolled oats, one-for-one, for any of these ingredients.

Cooking Hints and Safety Tips (please review pages 11–15)

- Ultraclean hands today! Keep damp paper towels handy.
- Spraying the baking tray with nonstick spray is an adult job, but kids can "help." An adult should hold the can and aim, and a child can press the button. If the spray lands all in one place, just rub it around with a paper towel.
- Lightly spray the measuring cup with nonstick spray before measuring the honey. Don't worry too much about the exact measurement.
- Take the stress out of measuring liquids by placing the measuring cup in a pie pan. Let your child pour or spoon the oil and honey into the measuring cup. The pie pan will catch the spills.

- ✦ The mixture is quite sticky. The kids might want to flour their hands ("wash hands with flour") or have their palms covered with a light coating of nonstick spray.
- ✦ Putting the tray into the oven and taking it out are adult jobs! Let the granola cool down before adding the dried fruit and serving.
- ✦ Store the granola in a tightly closed jar in the freezer for maximum freshness. (This recipe fits nicely into two 10-ounce jars.)

Children's Tools: Large bowl; dry measuring cups; measuring spoons; 2-cup-capacity liquid measuring cup; small whisk; rubber spatula; 13- by 18-inch baking tray (or 2 smaller trays); a bowl and spoon for each person

Crunchy Fruity Granola Recipe

Nonstick spray for the baking tray and honey measuring cup

3 cups rolled oats

2 cups combined seeds and chopped nuts

1/2 teaspoon salt

1/3 cup brown sugar

3/4 cup canola oil

1/2 cup honey

1 tablespoon vanilla extract

1 cup assorted dried fruit (small varieties, such as raisins, currants, cranberries, or blueberries)

1) Preheat the oven to 325°F. Spray a 13- by 18-inch baking tray with nonstick spray.
2) Combine the oats, seeds and chopped nuts, salt, and brown sugar in a large bowl.
3) Combine the oil, honey, and vanilla extract in 2-cup liquid measuring cup, and pour this into the dry ingredients. Mix thoroughly and spread on the prepared tray.
4) Bake for 30 minutes, or until golden. (Stir it once or twice during baking.)
5) Cool on the tray. When it has cooled down and become crunchy, add the dried fruit.
6) Eat plain or with milk.

NOTE: The combined seeds and chopped nuts can be sunflower seeds, sesame seeds, pumpkin seeds, almonds, pecans, walnuts, or anything else you have on hand.

YIELD: 6 to 8 cups

Crunchy Fruity Granola

put 3 cups oats
in bowl

add 2 cups seeds
and nuts

add 1/2 teaspoon salt

add 1/3 cup brown sugar

mix with hands

put 3/4 cup oil in cup

add 1/2 cup honey

add 1 tablespoon
vanilla extract

whisk the wet

pour wet into dry

mix with hands

spread on tray

bake 30 minutes

add fruit

EAT!

The Critics Rave:

Peeling is like giving the cucumber a haircut. —ZACHARY

This can be a drinking soup instead of the spoon kind. —MIA

That was a good snack! I liked the mint. —NATE

More please! I really liked it. —ANDREW

To the Grown-ups:

Try this unusual cold soup on a hot summer day. The kids might be skeptical at first, but as they hunker down and begin peeling the cucumbers, they will become more and more interested in the project.

We normally think of mint as the flavor of our toothpaste or as a kind of candy. But kids are fascinated to learn that mint is actually a plant with small green leaves that can be chopped up and used to season other foods—even things that are not sweet! Give your children a few sprigs of fresh mint and let them take off the leaves and count them. You can tell them that plants whose leaves are used to season things are called "herbs." And mint is the most refreshing herb of all.

Cooking Hints and Safety Tips (please review pages 11–15):

- Peeling the cucumbers is a real focal point for the kids. (Later, the hunt for peels in far corners of your kitchen can be a fun project unto itself.)
- Take the stress out of measuring yogurt by putting the measuring cup in a pie pan. Let your child pour or spoon the yogurt into the measuring cup. The pie pan will catch the spills.

- Lightly spray the teaspoon with nonstick spray before measuring the honey. Don't worry too much about the exact measurement.
- Kids can push the buttons on the blender. (It's easiest for them to use their thumbs.) With a little adult assistance, they can also pour the soup out of the blender. It must be made very clear that they should never touch the blade.
- If you intend to serve this in drinking cups, make sure the purée is very smooth. If you will be using bowls and spoons, it's okay to leave some small pieces.

Children's Tools: Vegetable peeler; cutting boards and child-appropriate knives; blender; 1- or 2-cup-capacity liquid measuring cup; measuring spoons; a bowl and spoon or a drinking cup for each person

Cool Cucumber Soup Recipe

2 medium cucumbers
1 cup plain yogurt
10 leaves fresh mint
Nonstick spray for the honey spoon
2 teaspoons honey
1/4 teaspoon salt

1) Peel the cucumbers, then cut them down the center lengthwise. Use a spoon to scrape out the seeds. (It's easiest to do this right over, and into, the garbage.)
2) Cut the cucumbers into large chunks.
3) Place the cucumber in the blender with the yogurt, mint, honey, and salt, and purée until smooth—or mostly smooth.
4) Serve cold, in bowls with spoons or in cups for drinking. Eat or drink!

NOTE: This soup stratifies if kept in the refrigerator for more than a day. To reblend, just shake the container or stir from the bottom.

YIELD: 3 to 4 servings (2 cups total)

Cool Cucumber Soup

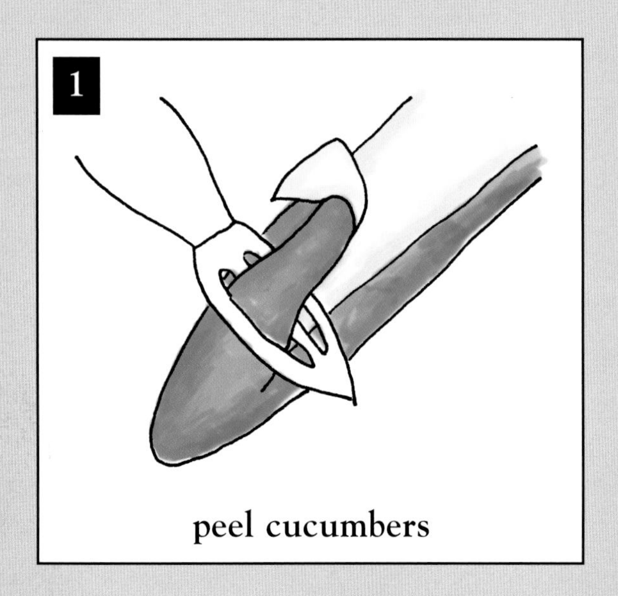

peel cucumbers

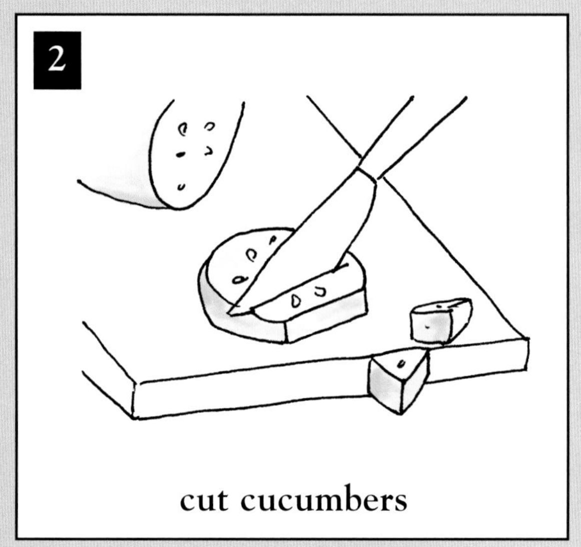

cut cucumbers

put in blender

add 1 cup yogurt

add 10 mint leaves

add 2 teaspoons honey

add 1/4 teaspoon salt

blend

pour

EAT or DRINK!

The Critics Rave:

Look at! The carrot goes in the hole and it makes little pieces! —ETHAN

That cabbage is purple inside! —SASCHA

That's not lettuce—it's cabbage! —GABRIELLE

It's like raisin bran, except it's salad. —SARAH

To the Grown-ups:

I was amazed to discover that preschool children really like cole slaw. The vibrant colors of this version, punctuated by the ever-appreciated presence of raisins, make the project even more interesting.

You can let the kids "help" with the vegetable preparation by giving them small pieces to cut even smaller with child-appropriate knives. This is optional. The main vegetable-cutting focus in this recipe is simply grating the carrot, which is a very big deal to little children. When you get near the end of the carrot, suggest that your child snack on the final piece rather than grating it all the way down.

Cooking Hints and Safety Tips (please review pages 11–15):

- ✦ Make sure the carrot is at least an inch in diameter, as larger carrots are safer to grate. Closely supervise the grating, telling your child how it works, and warning about the sharp edges: "Be careful of your knuckles." Younger children may need you to guide their hand up and down—or they might want you to do it altogether.

- ✦ To make things easier, you can have the kids measure the dressing ingredients into a 2-cup-capacity liquid measuring cup with a pouring spout, mix it there, and then pour it into the salad.
- ✦ Lightly spray the teaspoon with nonstick spray before measuring the honey. Don't worry too much about the exact measurement.

Children's Tools: Cutting boards and child-appropriate knives (if the children will help with the cutting); large bowl; dry measuring cups; standing grater with large holes; 1- or 2-cup-capacity liquid measuring cup; measuring spoons; small whisk; long-handled wooden spoon; a plate and fork for each person

Rainbow-Raisin Cole Slaw Recipe

1 1/2 cups (packed) shredded green cabbage
1 1/2 cups (packed) shredded purple cabbage
1/2 small red bell pepper, minced or cut in thin slices
1/2 small yellow bell pepper, minced or cut in thin slices
1 medium carrot, grated
1/2 cup raisins (black or golden, or both)
1/3 cup mayonnaise
1/3 cup plain yogurt
Nonstick spray for the honey spoon
1 tablespoon honey
1 teaspoon cider vinegar
1/2 teaspoon salt

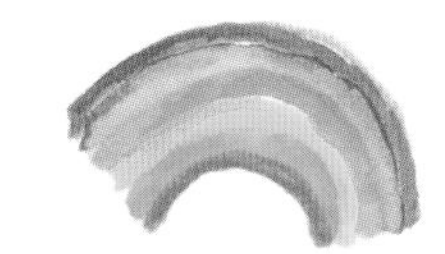

1) Combine the vegetables and raisins in a large bowl.
2) In a second container, combine the mayonnaise, yogurt, honey, vinegar, and salt. Use a fork or small whisk to mix until uniform ("until you don't see the honey anymore").
3) Pour the dressing into the salad, mix well, and then eat!

YIELD: 4 to 6 servings

Rainbow-Raisin Cole Slaw

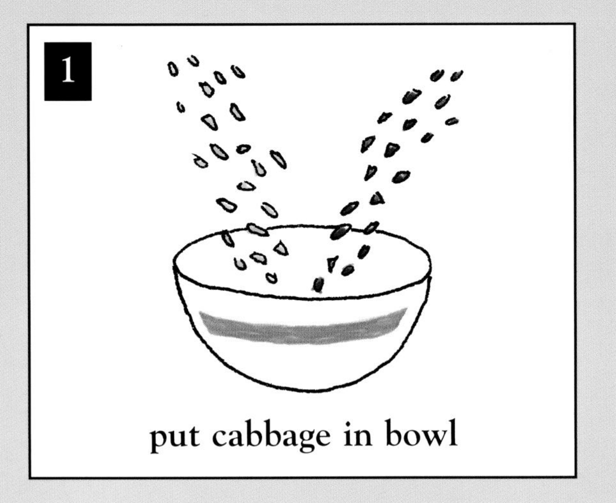

put cabbage in bowl

add peppers

grate carrot

put carrot in bowl

add raisins

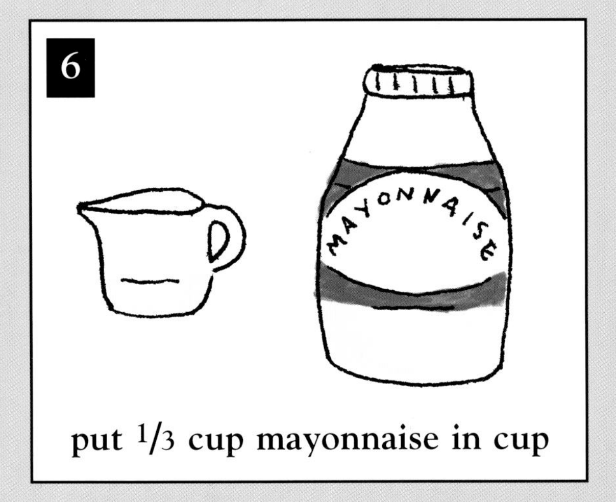

put 1/3 cup mayonnaise in cup

add 1/3 cup yogurt

8 add 1 tablespoon honey

9 add 1 teaspoon vinegar

10 add 1/2 teaspoon salt

11 whisk dressing

12 pour dressing

13 stir

14 EAT!

The Critics Rave:

I covered a rosemary with some dough. It's gonna be hiding. —JACK

Now it's all painted. —SIMONE

I want to have about nine pieces. —CHARLEY

Hey! Wanna taste these green things? —HAIYAN

To the Grown-ups:

This is a wonderful bread-baking experience that will make your house smell good for hours!

Focaccia is made from the same dough as pizza, only it is thicker and shaped into a rectangle instead of a circle. It is baked with no cheese or other toppings, just olive oil and a sprinkling of rosemary and salt.

You'll be buying premade dough, so that all the kids need to do is shape it and add the olive oil, rosemary, and salt.

Yeasted dough stretches most easily when it has been resting for a good while (at least 15 minutes past its last handling), so my basic instruction for this recipe is to simply have the dough on hand, remove it from the package, and, with no kneading whatsoever, transfer the risen dough to the prepared baking tray. The finished "look" can be very rough-hewn—it really doesn't matter!

Cooking Hints and Safety Tips (please review pages 11–15):

- ✦ Ultraclean hands today!
- ✦ Keep damp paper towels handy.
- ✦ Spray the kids' hands with nonstick spray for easiest dough handling.

- ✦ Spraying the baking tray—and the kids' hands—with nonstick spray is an adult job, but kids can "help." An adult should hold the can and aim, and a child can press the button. If the spray lands all in one place, just rub it around with a paper towel.
- ✦ "Painting" with olive oil is fun, and the children will want to take a good, long time with it. They might also want to smooth on the olive oil with their hands. This is very sensual!
- ✦ The rosemary should be crumbled quite small, as it is a tough, woody herb. If you are using fresh rosemary, the kids can help strip the leaves from the stems, and then an adult should chop it quite fine with a good, sharp knife.
- ✦ Be sure to remind them to "sprinkle the rosemary in different places," so it gets fairly evenly distributed.
- ✦ Putting the tray into the oven and taking it out—and then removing the focaccia from the pan—are adult jobs!

Children's Tools: 13- by 18-inch baking tray; pastry brush; small bowl with olive oil; a plate for each person

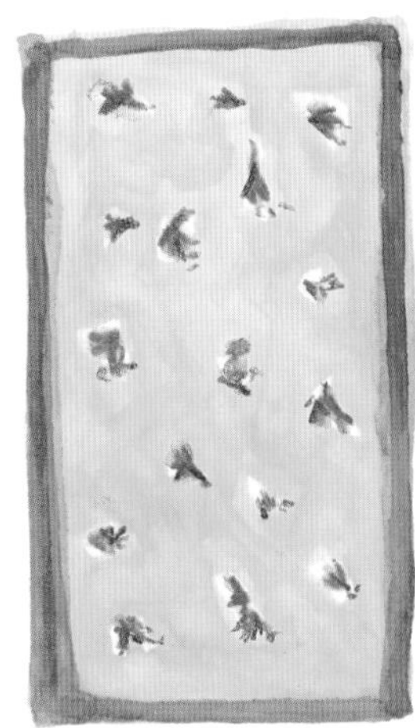

Focaccia Recipe

1 1/2 pounds storebought pizza dough
Nonstick spray for hands and baking tray
1/4 cup olive oil
3 tablespoons minced rosemary (fresh or dried)
1 to 2 tablespoons kosher salt

1) Preheat the oven to 450°F and spray a 13- by 18-inch baking tray with nonstick spray. Add the storebought dough, straight from its package, and push and stretch it into a rectangle about 10 by 15 inches.
2) Brush generously with olive oil and sprinkle with the minced rosemary.
3) Bake in the center of the oven for 15 minutes, or until lightly brown on both the bottom and the top.
4) Remove from the oven and cool on a rack for at least 15 minutes, then let the children brush on more olive oil and sprinkle with a little kosher salt.
5) Eat!

YIELD: One 10- by 15-inch rectangle

Focaccia

put dough on tray

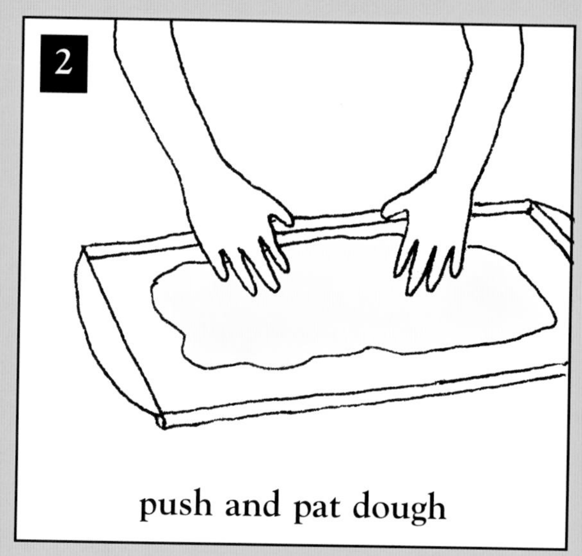

push and pat dough

paint with olive oil

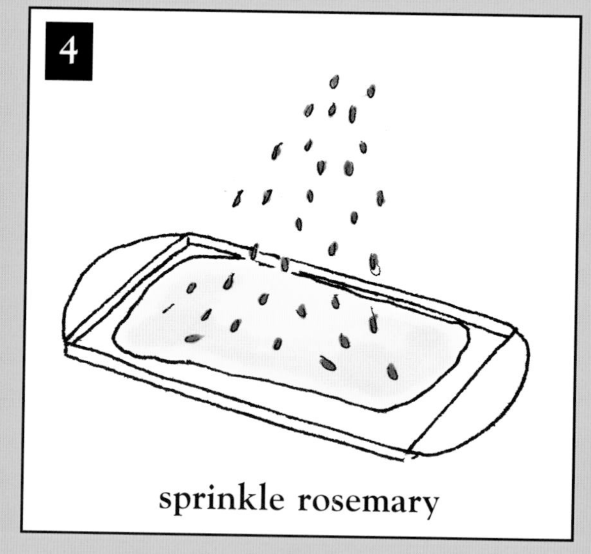

sprinkle rosemary

5

bake 15 minutes

6

paint with more olive oil

7

sprinkle with salt

8

EAT!

The Critics Rave:

It was so funny! The zucchini plopped into there! And I pulled it out and I ate it! —ETHAN

Put in the part that's not the stem. —NATE

This is what parents do at grown-up parties. They stand around and they dip food and they talk. —GABRIELLE

I need to go home and buy vegetables with my mom. —LEAH

To the Grown-ups:

This thick green dip made from fresh herbs and ricotta cheese is the perfect way to inspire children to vegetable appreciation. Children love to scoop it up with crunchy sugar snap peas, small zucchini spears, sweet bell pepper pieces, and baby carrots. After kids make the dip, they can take their time making an artful arrangement of vegetables and then, after a dramatic moment of presentation, literally dig in.

Let the kids sniff the fresh herbs one at a time, so they can become familiar with the lovely aromas. A good way to do this is to have them rub a leaf with their fingers and then sniff their fingers.

Cooking Hints and Safety Tips (please review pages 11–15):

- An effective and satisfying way to remove garlic skin is to put the clove on a cutting board and let your child smash it with a can of soup.

✦ Kids can push the buttons on the food processor. (It's easiest for them to use their thumbs.) They can also scrape out the dip with a rubber spatula once the blade has been removed. It must be made very clear that they should never touch the blade.

✦ Take the stress out of measuring liquids by placing the measuring cup in a pie pan. Let your child pour the buttermilk into the measuring cup. (For a very small child, pour the buttermilk into a small pitcher first.) The pie pan will catch the spills.

✦ Even though this recipe uses only a teaspoon of lemon juice, it's fun to set up a citrus juicer and let your child squeeze the juice. It's quite challenging for a small child to squeeze a lemon, so be sure to provide a guiding hand and lots of elbow room.

✦ Lightly spray the teaspoon with nonstick spray before measuring the honey. Don't worry too much about the exact measurement.

Children's Tools: Can of soup (for smashing garlic); food processor; dry measuring cups; 2-cup-capacity liquid measuring cup; measuring spoons; citrus juicer; salt shaker; rubber spatula; serving bowl; serving plate

Green Garden Dip Recipe

1 small clove garlic

1 cup coarsely chopped parsley (large stems removed; smaller stems okay)

4 scallions, trimmed of roots and cut into 1-inch pieces (white and green parts)

15 basil leaves (no stems)

3 small fresh dill sprigs, about 2 inches long

3/4 cup buttermilk

1 1/2 cups ricotta cheese

1 teaspoon fresh lemon juice

Nonstick spray for the honey spoon

1 teaspoon honey

6 shakes salt

Vegetables for dipping

1) Smash and peel the garlic. Place the garlic, parsley, scallions, basil, and dill in a food processor. Turn on to pulverize. Stop the machine and remove the top.
2) Add the buttermilk, ricotta, lemon juice, honey, and salt. Close the top and run the machine until everything is blended.
3) Transfer to a bowl, and serve surrounded by an assortment of vegetables.

YIELD: About 2 cups dip

Green Garden Dip

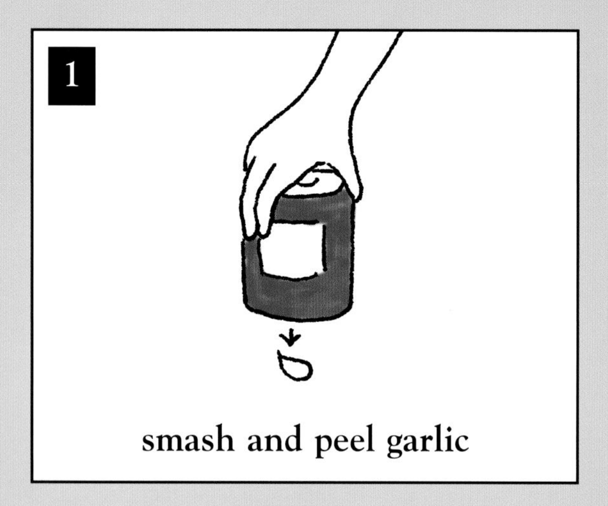

smash and peel garlic

put garlic in blender

add 1 cup parsley

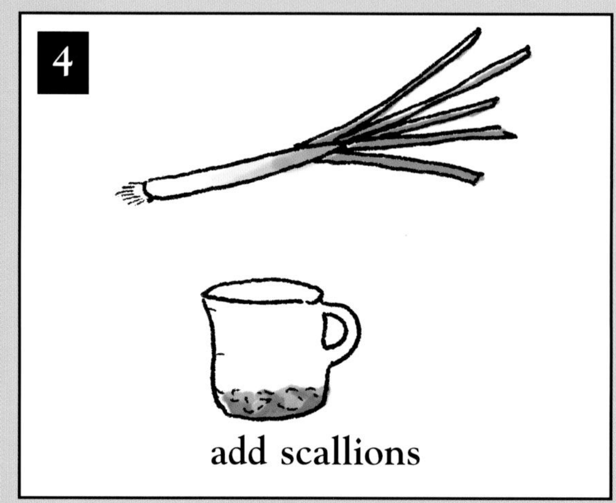

add scallions

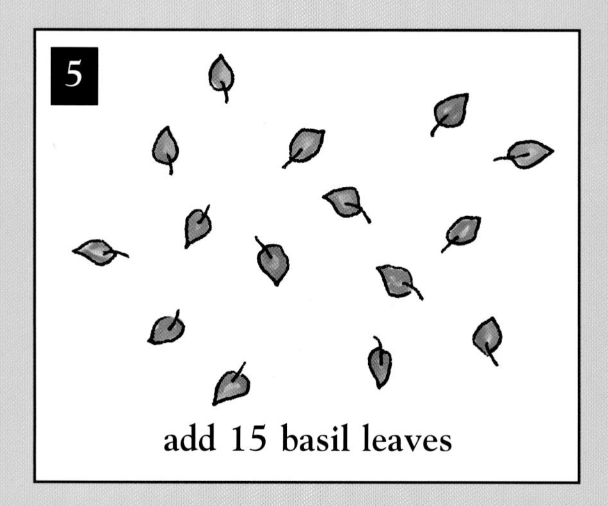

add 15 basil leaves

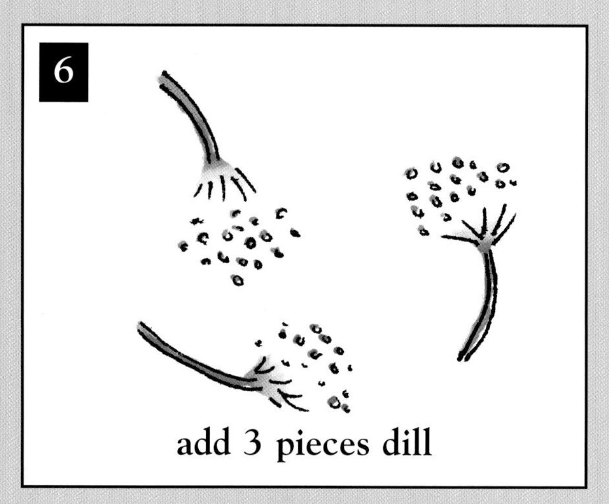

add 3 pieces dill

blend

add 3/4 cup buttermilk

add 1 1/2 cups ricotta

add 1 teaspoon lemon juice

add 1 teaspoon honey

add 6 shakes salt

blend

dip and EAT!

The Critics Rave:

I don't know if I like all these things, but I'll put them in anyway. —LEAH

I have soup very often because my dad slays dragons. —JACK

I like the broth and the letters and the peas. —SERAFINA

I made the green bean into nine green beans with my knife. —CHARLEY

To the Grown-ups:

Kids appreciate being given the space to approach vegetables on their own—to be *pulled*, rather than pushed, into the relationship. This lively soup is an appealing opportunity to do just that. With an approach similar to that of Polka Dot Rice and the salad bar in *Pretend Soup*, this project is set up on a table with a variety of vegetables, diced tofu, and cooked alphabet noodles in separate containers. The children then fill their individual bowls with the components of their choice, and the adult ladles in the broth. The soup makes itself right in the bowl! The kids get to count, rather than measure, the accoutrements, which provides them with a fun math exercise at the same time. If your child doesn't want to include all the options, that's fine.

Cooking Hints and Safety Tips (please review pages 11–15):

- Cutting the green beans and tofu—and grating the carrot—are not part of the basic child recipe, but if the children are interested in participating, by all means let them. Steam or blanch the green beans ahead of time, so they will be softer and thus easier for the kids to cut with their child-appropriate knives. Tofu is a cinch for kids to cut.

- ✦ If the kids are going to grate the carrot, make sure it is at least an inch in diameter. Larger carrots are safer to grate. Closely supervise the grating, telling your child how it works and warning about the sharp edges. "Be careful of your knuckles!" is an important instruction. Younger children may need you to guide their hand up and down—or they might want you to do it altogether.
- ✦ Only an adult should handle or serve the heated broth. For safety's sake, it needs to be only warm enough to heat up the room-temperature vegetables, tofu, and noodles.

Children's Tools: Cutting boards and child-appropriate knives (if the kids will be cutting); medium-sized bowls (one for each soup ingredient and one for each person); a spoon for each person

Counting Soup Recipe

2 cups peas, fresh and lightly steamed, or frozen

2 cups corn, fresh and uncooked, or frozen

2 cups diced tofu

2 cups grated carrot

1/3 pound green beans, cut into 1-inch pieces and steamed or blanched until tender

2 cups cooked alphabet noodles (2/3 cup uncooked, boiled until tender and drained)

4 cups vegetable broth, heated

1) If you are using frozen peas or corn, place each in a strainer or a colander and run under room-temperature tap water to thaw. Drain thoroughly and transfer to separate bowls.
2) Place all the ingredients except the broth in separate bowls. Arrange them on the table in the following order: tofu, carrots, peas, corn, green beans, noodles. Place a regular dinner spoon (nothing larger) in each bowl.
3) Let the children go through the lineup with a medium-sized soup bowl, counting in the prescribed number of spoonfuls of each ingredient.
4) Ladle warm broth over the top, and eat!

NOTE: There are some very good varieties of vegetable broth available in supermarkets. I prefer Imagine brand, which comes unrefrigerated in a 1-quart box (like soymilk).

YIELD: 4 to 6 servings

Counting Soup

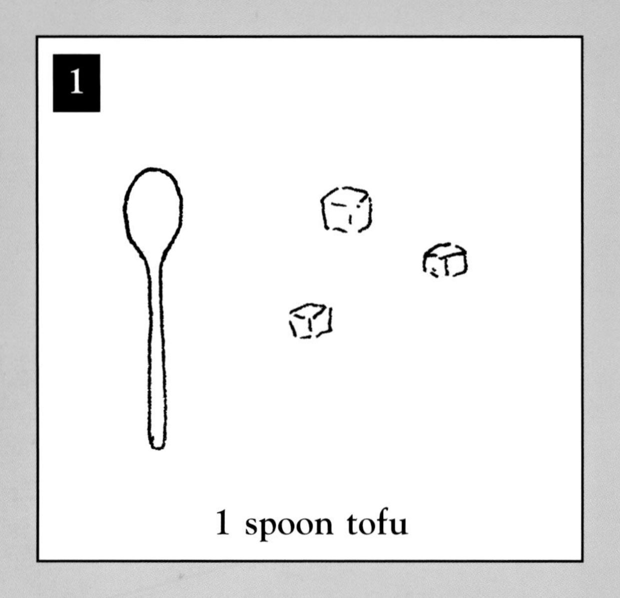

1 spoon tofu

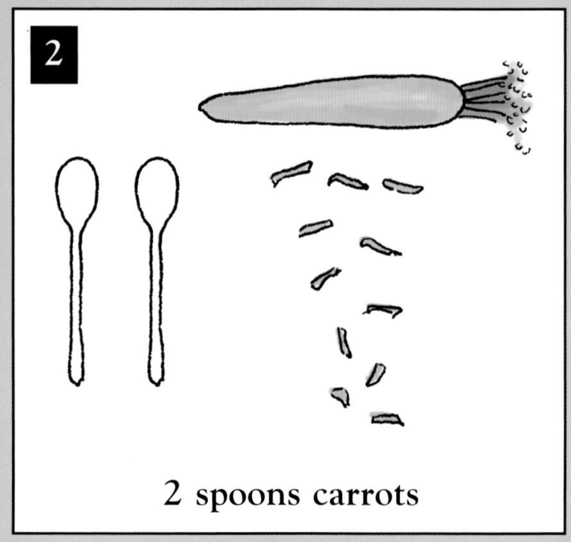

2 spoons carrots

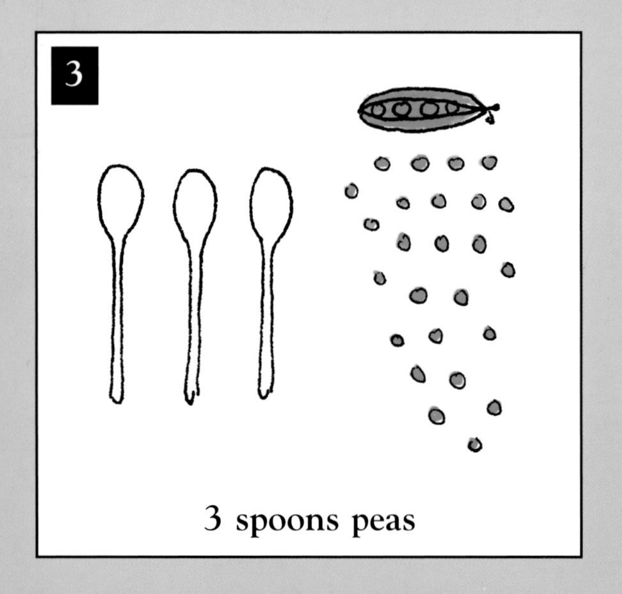

3 spoons peas

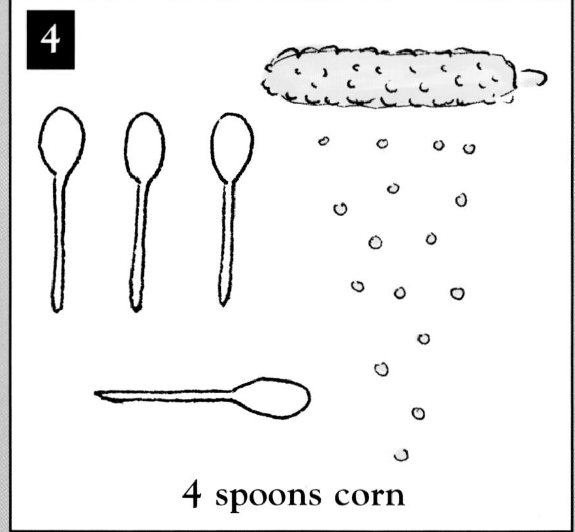

4 spoons corn

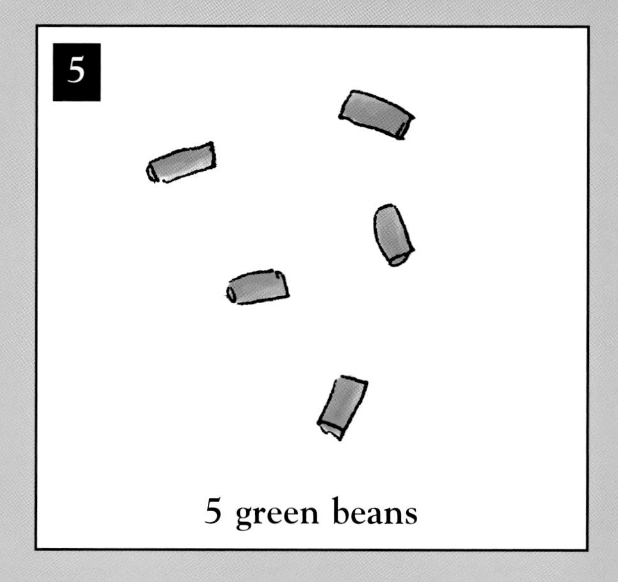

5 green beans

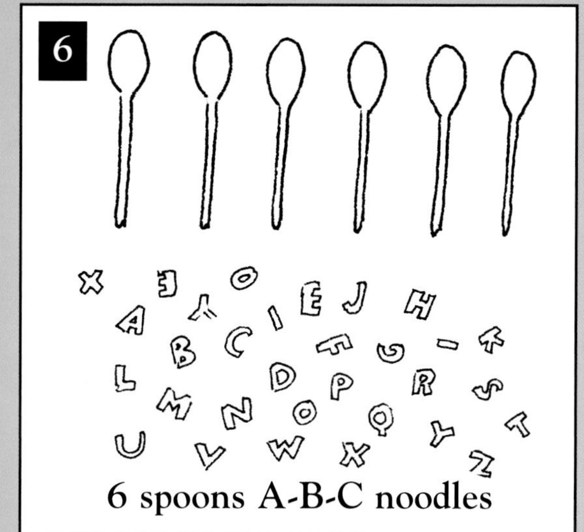

6 spoons A-B-C noodles

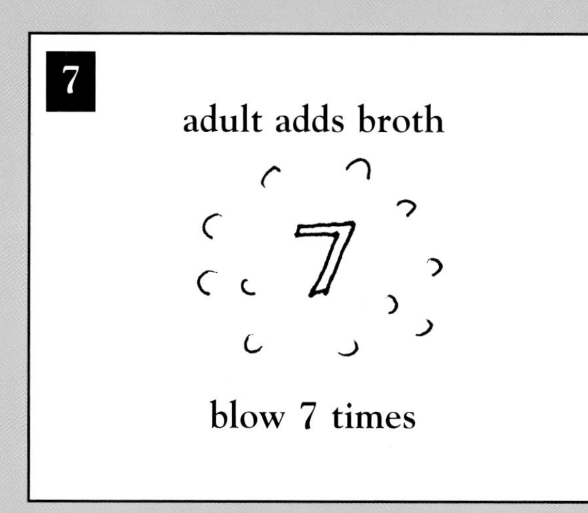

blow 7 times

stir 8 times

EAT!

The Critics Rave:

This shaker is working! I shaked the cinnamon! —ZACHARY

I hear the bubbles! I can hear bubbling! —GABRIELLE

Oh let me smell that yummy cinnamon! —RAYMOND

To the Grown-ups:

Sweet potatoes are a supernutritious food, packing in a big dose of beta-carotene and lots of healthy fiber. Here, children get to experience this potent orange vegetable prepared with minimal seasoning—a light touch of butter and just a touch of honey, plus the natural sweetness of apples and cinnamon. They won't miss the marshmallows!

A fantastic scent hits the air when cinnamon is added to melted butter in a hot pan. This is one of those dramatic kitchen moments that children talk about for days and remember for years. Cooking apples in the cinnamon butter is very satisfying, and so is mashing the components together. Note that, although it is not part of the official child recipe, the kids can help cut apples and squeeze the lemon juice.

Cooking Hints and Safety Tips (please review pages 11–15):

- Use a very large bowl for this, and encourage your young chef to mash slowly. If the bowl is placed on a low enough surface, the kids can use their body weight to bear down while mashing or, in their words, as they "squish and turn."
- It's easiest for the kids to mash the sweet potatoes while they are still warm (or warmed up in a microwave). Just be sure they are not too hot.
- The amount of butter is approximate. "Two slices" is the child's instruction, and if you leave the calibrated wrapper on, your child can simply cut the slices through the paper at 1-tablespoon intervals (or thereabouts) and then remove the wrapper.

- ✦ Use a soft, sweet variety of apple, like McIntosh or Gravenstein.
- ✦ Add the cooked apples to the sweet potatoes as a team: The adult holds the pan and tilts it into the bowl, and the young chef scrapes it in.
- ✦ Use a salt shaker that is neither too fast nor too slow.
- ✦ Lightly spray the teaspoon with nonstick spray before measuring the honey. Don't worry too much about the exact measurement.

Children's Tools: Large bowl; potato masher; cutting boards and child-appropriate knives; medium-sized skillet; measuring spoons; long-handled wooden spoon; salt shaker; a plate and fork for each person

Sweet Potato Surprise Recipe

1 1/2 pounds sweet potatoes
2 tablespoons unsalted butter
1/2 teaspoon cinnamon
3/4 pound apples, peeled, cored, and sliced
6 shakes salt
Nonstick spray for the honey spoon
1 tablespoon honey
2 teaspoons fresh lemon juice

1) Cut the unpeeled sweet potatoes into 1 1/2-inch chunks.
2) Cook the sweet potatoes in a steamer over simmering water until very tender and easily pierced with a fork (about 20 minutes). Cool the potatoes until comfortable to handle, then peel by hand or with a paring knife. Transfer the peeled sweet potatoes to a large bowl, and mash.
3) Add the butter to a heated skillet over medium heat, and let the kids watch it melt. Sprinkle in the cinnamon and then add the apples. Stir and cook until the apples are very soft. Scrape them into the sweet potatoes.
4) Add the salt, honey, and lemon juice, and mash again. You can keep working it until very smooth, or leave some texture—it's fine either way.

YIELD: 4 to 5 servings

Sweet Potato Surprise

mash sweet potatoes in a bowl

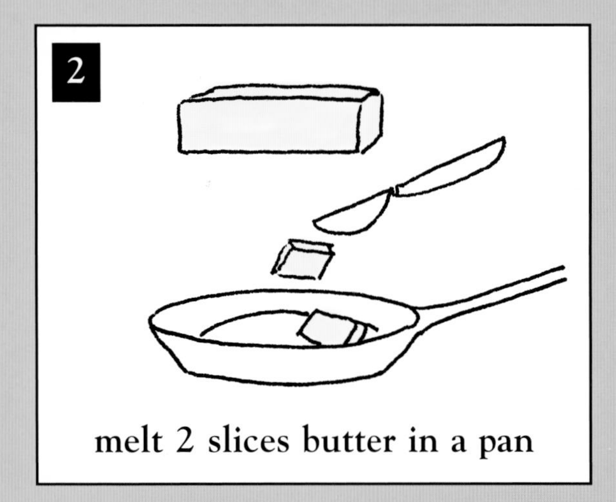

melt 2 slices butter in a pan

sprinkle 1/2 teaspoon cinnamon

add apples

stir and cook

add apples to sweet potatoes

add 6 shakes salt

add 1 tablespoon honey

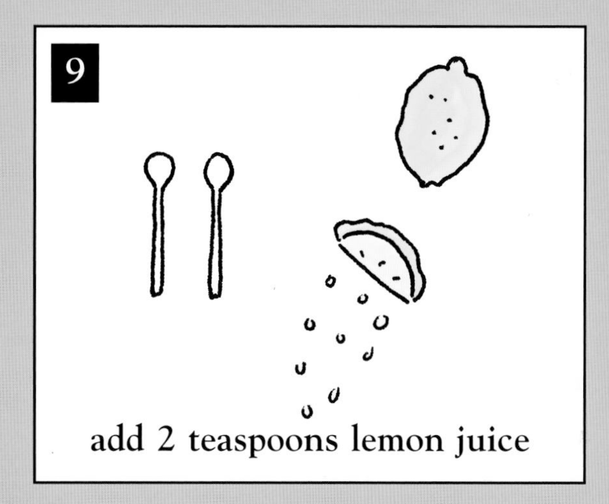

add 2 teaspoons lemon juice

mash

EAT!

The Critics Rave:

If you lick your fingers, they'll taste sour. —MAX

It's not lemonade yet, because it doesn't have all that other stuff in it. —ELLA

The syrup is the best part! And the cranberry juice! And the lemons! —CHARLEY

To the Grown-ups:

This version of lemonade, magical to kids, invites young chefs to use some muscle and squeeze the lemons by hand. The unusual part comes when they spoon in the cranberry concentrate and watch the "sun" rise. The kids will want to stir a lot, and rather than drink from the glass, they might prefer a spoon, which lends a sense of ritual.

If you use a juicer with a clear bottom, the kids will enjoy viewing the accumulation of juice. This provides some helpful encouragement for their earnest squeezing efforts.

This recipe is sweetened with a syrup that you make ahead of time. "Simple syrup," as it is known in culinary dialect, is a solution of water and sugar that blends in perfectly when you want a touch of sweetness with no additional texture. If you have extra syrup and lemon juice left over after this project, store them in separate, labeled jars in the refrigerator for another time.

Cooking Hints and Safety Tips (please review pages 11–15):

- The recipe calls for 2 tablespoons fresh lemon juice per serving. I recommend that you have the children squeeze at least 3 or 4 lemons and then measure out each portion as needed.
- Only an adult should cut the lemons.

- ✦ Save this recipe for a time when your child's hands are free of cuts or "owies."
- ✦ Hold the juicer steady while your child pushes and twists the lemons. For maximum leverage, put the juicer on a low surface, so your young chef can bear down with full body weight while "turning and pushing with two hands."
- ✦ Frozen cranberry juice concentrate should be a little firm for digging up with a spoon; young children may need help scooping it out.

Children's Tools: Citrus juice squeezer (manual—with a clear glass or plastic bottom, if possible); measuring spoons; clear drinking glass

Sunrise Lemonade Recipe

2 tablespoons fresh lemon juice

3 tablespoons simple syrup (recipe follows)

3/4 cup water

1 tablespoon frozen cranberry juice concentrate (partially defrosted)

3 ice cubes

1) Squeeze the lemons on a juice squeezer.
2) Measure 2 tablespoons of the juice into a clear drinking glass.
3) Measure in the simple syrup.
4) Measure in the water; stir.
5) Add the frozen concentrate. It will sink to the bottom of the glass. Stir gently from the bottom to create a "sunrise" effect, then add ice cubes and drink!

YIELD: 1 serving

SIMPLE SYRUP RECIPE

1/2 cup sugar

1/2 cup water

1) Combine the sugar and water in a small saucepan.
2) Cook over medium heat, stirring occasionally, until the sugar is completely dissolved.
3) Cool at least to room temperature before using.

YIELD: 1/2 cup

Sunrise Lemonade

squeeze lemons

pour 2 tablespoons lemon juice into glass

add 3 tablespoons syrup

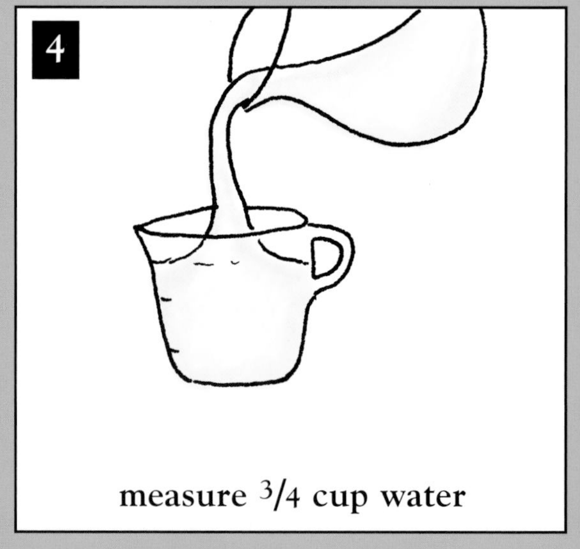

measure 3/4 cup water

5
pour into glass

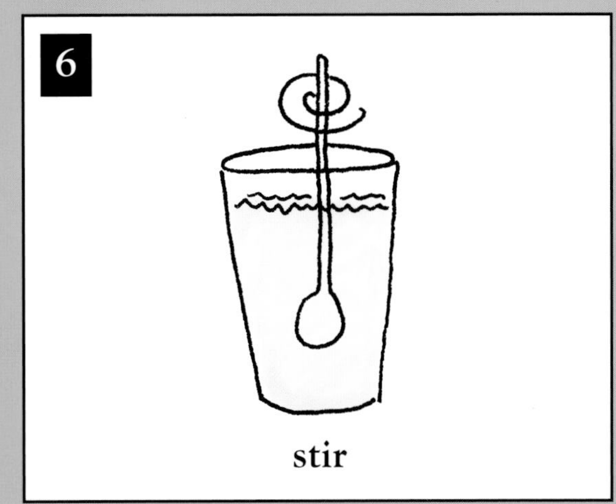
6
stir

7
add 1 tablespoon
frozen cranberry juice

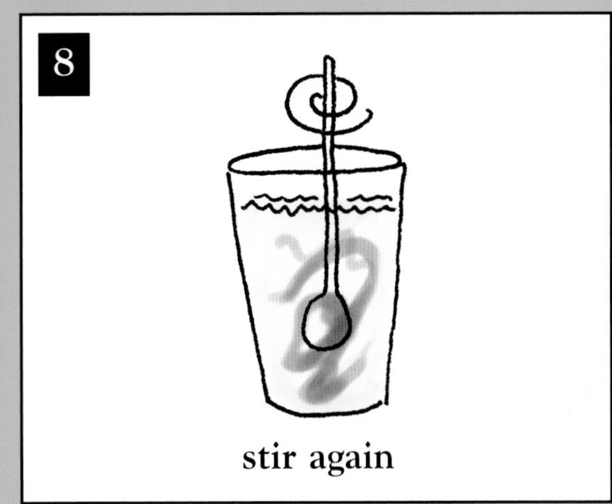
8
stir again

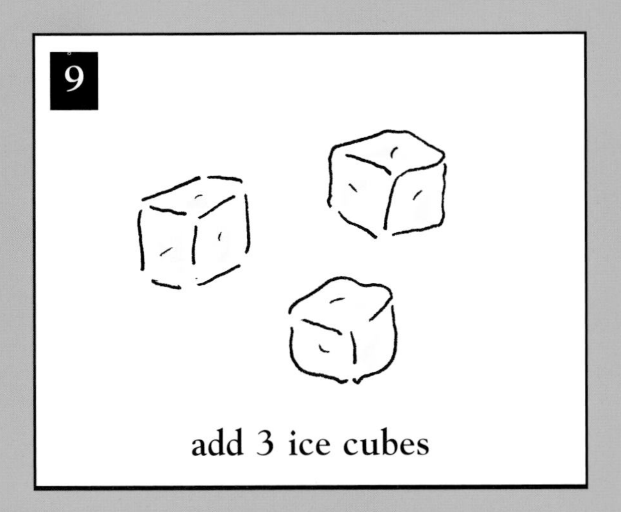
9
add 3 ice cubes

10
DRINK!

The Critics Rave:

Carrots are hard to cut. Sometimes you just have to break them. —SARAH JANE

The rice was hard, but you cooked it and then it was soft, right? —LEAH

When you put in less rice and more vegetables, it has more colors. —MOLLY

When you put in the soy sauce it turns dark, and then when you mix it in it gets light again. —SIMONE

To the Grown-ups:

Rice is a great vehicle for bringing together children and vegetables. The trick is to choose a colorful assortment of vegetables and then to cut the larger ones into very small pieces, so that, together, it all looks like confetti—or in this case, polka dots. It works best if you set out the rice and vegetables in different bowls, as you would for a salad bar, and let each child prepare his or her individual portion. They may put in only a few of the options for their first helping, but when it comes time for seconds (which you can count on), the kids might want to expand their horizons by a vegetable or two. (They are attracted to the colors and are also intrigued by what the other kids are choosing, if you do this in a group.) Adding the soy sauce is a point of great interest. Children like to observe the way it disappears into the rice.

Cooking Hints and Safety Tips (please review pages 11–15):

- Cook the rice well ahead of time, then let it cool down so the children are working with rice that is either warm or at room temperature. The vegetables should be at room temperature too, so take them out of the refrigerator several hours in advance of the project.

- ✦ You can augment or replace the rice with other cooked grains, such as millet or barley. This becomes a good way to gently introduce whole grains to children (and to big persons as well).
- ✦ Cutting the vegetables is not part of the basic child recipe, but if the children are interested in participating, by all means let them. Steam or blanch the broccoli and carrots ahead of time, so they will be softer and thus easier for the kids to cut with their child-appropriate knives.
- ✦ Make sure the soy sauce is in a shaker bottle that doesn't pour too quickly. Each shake should yield just a drop or two.

Children's Tools: Cutting boards and child-appropriate knives (if the kids will be cutting); medium-sized bowls (one for each vegetable and one for each person); spoons

Polka Dot Rice Recipe

1 1/2 cups uncooked long-grain brown rice (plain or basmati)

2 1/2 cups water

2 cups peas, fresh and lightly steamed, or frozen

2 cups corn, fresh and uncooked, or frozen

2 cups chopped broccoli, steamed or blanched until just tender

2 cups diced carrots, steamed or blanched until just tender

1/2 small red bell pepper, diced

2 scallions, trimmed of roots, sliced into thin rounds (whites and green parts)

Soy sauce

1) Combine the rice and water in a saucepan and bring to a boil. Turn the heat to the lowest simmer, cover the pot, and cook undisturbed for 40 minutes, or until the rice is tender. Remove from the heat and fluff with a fork to let the steam escape, and transfer to a bowl.
2) If you are using frozen peas or corn, place each in a strainer or a colander and run under room-temperature tap water to thaw. Drain thoroughly and transfer to separate bowls.
3) Place all the other vegetables in separate bowls.
4) Put a large spoonful of rice in a bowl, and customize with the vegetables. Sprinkle in a few drops of soy sauce, mix well , and eat!

YIELD: 5 or 6 servings

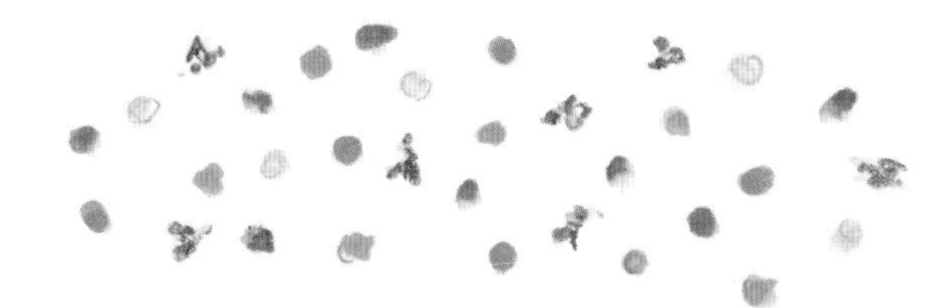

Polka Dot Rice

put rice in bowl

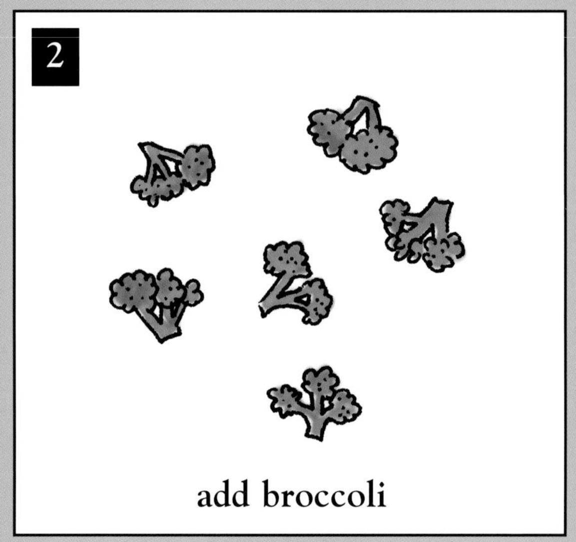

add broccoli

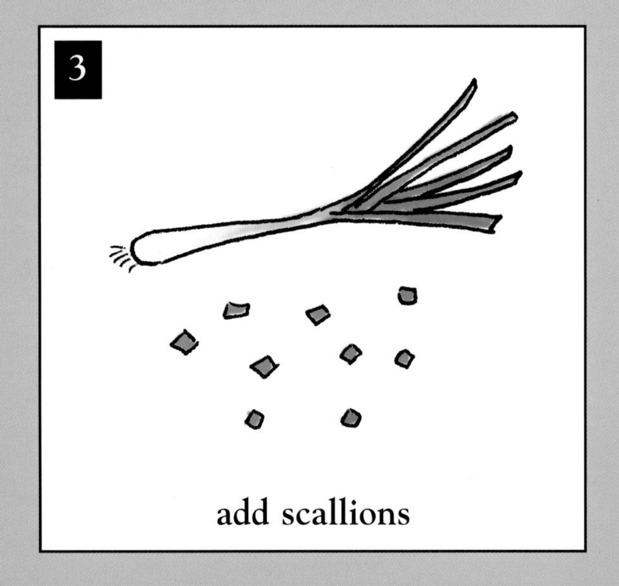

add scallions

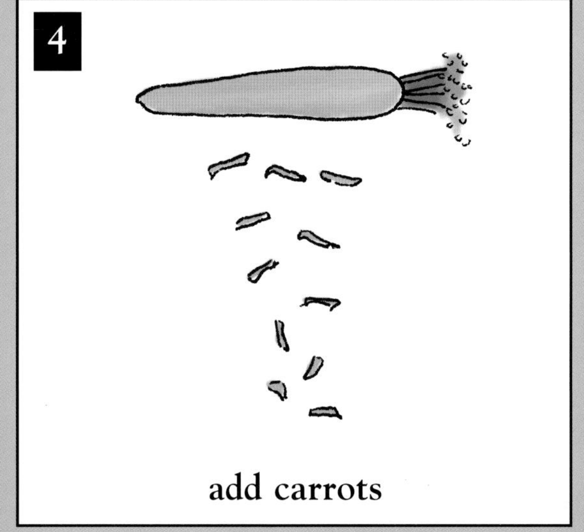

add carrots

5

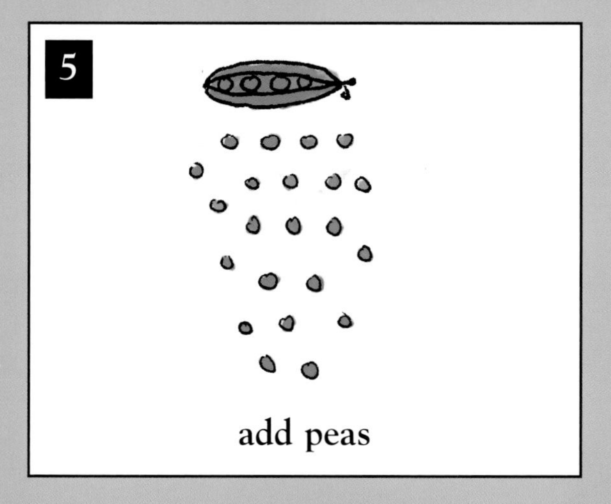

add peas

6

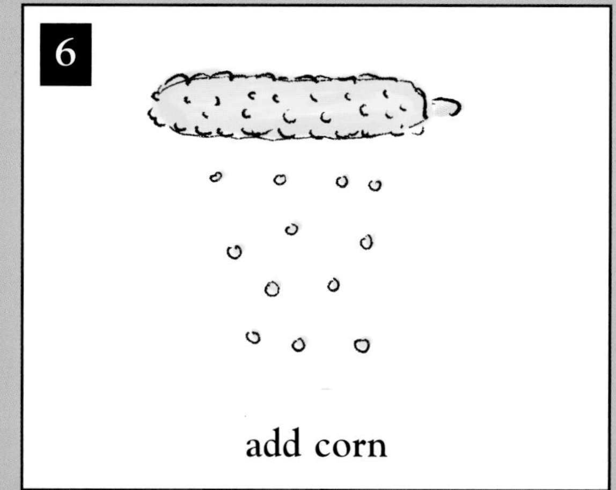

add corn

7

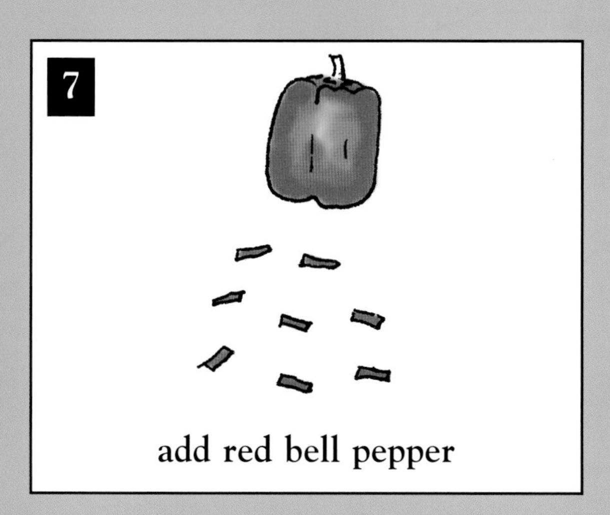

add red bell pepper

8

add 3 shakes soy sauce

9

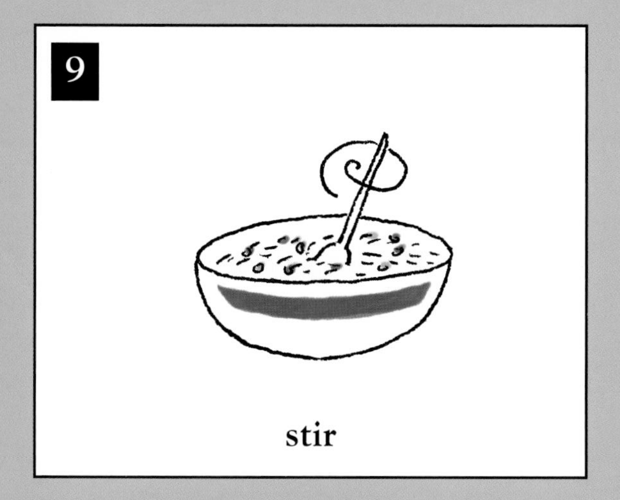

stir

10

EAT!

The Critics Rave:

The snow pea is a good scooper. —ELLA

Did you know that grasshoppers like snow peas? —CHARLEY

Be careful because this might be too yummy for me to eat! —THEO

I can't wait! —SASCHA

To the Grown-ups:

Children love this deeply flavored high-protein snack. They will enthusiastically scoop it up with carrots, celery, raw green beans, bell peppers, or snow peas—and will just as happily spread it on crackers.

Miso is a salty paste made from fermented soybeans and grains. You can find many different varieties of miso in natural food groceries and Asian markets (and in some regular supermarkets). For this recipe, use a variety that is mild in flavor, such as shiro, mellow white, or any miso that is very light in color.

When I first served this dip, already prepared, to a group of preschoolers, they recoiled from it, noting its brown color and suspicious, ambiguous identity (not their words). Then, a few days later, I brought in the unassembled ingredients, including the almonds and a blender to make our own almond butter, and this time the experience was completely different! Tasting one component at a time, the same children were enthralled with every step and each ingredient, discussing their impressions throughout the process. It was a real food literacy lesson! They loved the homemade almond butter so much that we had to make a second batch, because they'd consumed the entire first batch before we could get started on the bigger recipe.

Cooking Hints and Safety Tips (please review pages 11–15):

- ✦ If you prefer to make this recipe with commercially prepared almond butter, use 6 tablespoons; if it's salted, omit the salt from the recipe.
- ✦ Use a salt shaker that is neither too fast nor too slow.
- ✦ Kids can push the buttons on the blender. (It's easiest for them to use their thumbs.) However, removing the almond butter from the blender is an adult-only job. It must be made very clear that children should never touch the blade.
- ✦ Mixing this thick sauce is challenging for small children. Tell them to mix it by pushing it: "Mash down to the bowl."

Children's Tools: Dry measuring cup; blender; salt shaker; measuring spoons; medium-sized bowl; soup spoons for mashing

Miso-Almond Dipping Sauce Recipe

1 cup (1/4 pound) slivered almonds, lightly toasted

4 shakes salt

1 to 2 tablespoons oil (canola, peanut, or soy)

3 tablespoons shiro miso (or a similar light variety)

6 tablespoons warm apple juice

Vegetables for dipping or crackers for spreading

1) Place the almonds in a blender with the salt and 1 tablespoon of the oil.
2) Blend to make a smooth paste, adding another tablespoon of oil if necessary.
3) Transfer to a medium-sized bowl.
4) Add the miso and half the apple juice. Mash and stir until uniform.
5) Mix in the remaining apple juice. Serve at room temperature, with vegetables for dipping or spread on crackers.
6) Eat!

YIELD: 3 to 4 servings

Miso-Almond Dipping Sauce

put 1 cup almonds in blender

add 4 shakes salt

add 1 tablespoon oil

blend

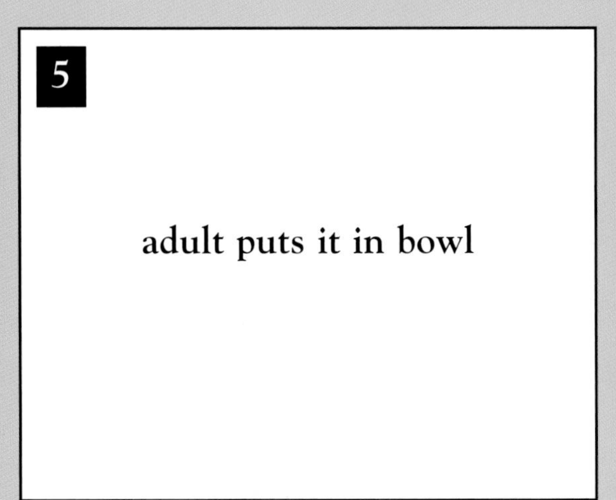

adult puts it in bowl

add 3 tablespoons miso

add 3 tablespoons apple juice

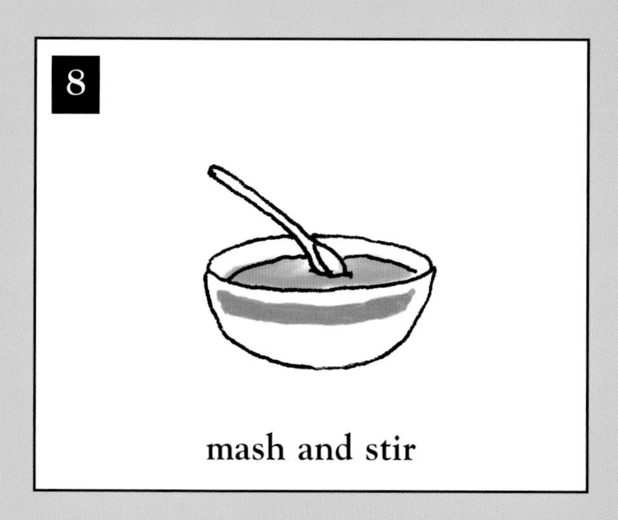

mash and stir

add 3 more tablespoons
apple juice

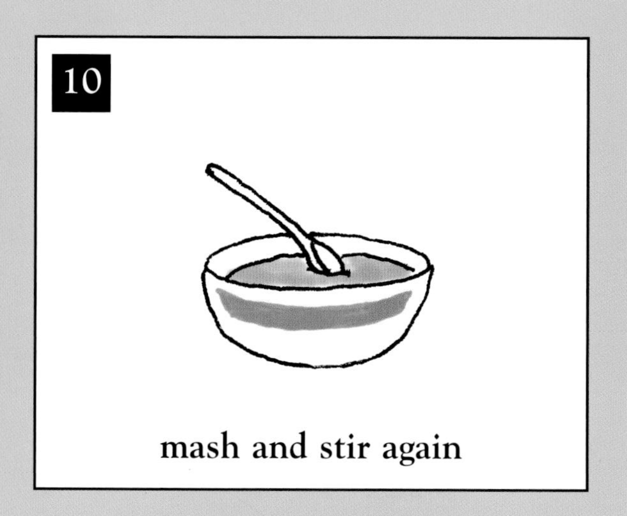

mash and stir again

dip and EAT!

The Critics Rave:

The butter gets flat and little. —GABRIELLE

Pass me that syrup! —REBECCA

Tomorrow we could make this again. —SARAH

To the Grown-ups:

Pancake batter is very inviting to small children—soft and easily mixed, yet sturdy enough to withstand enthusiasm. And it's so much fun to watch the change that takes place in the pan!

To simplify this recipe, make a dry pancake mix first. Then your child can finish the batter and cook the pancakes. (Seemingly mundane tasks like breaking eggs and beating with a whisk are especially interesting to young children.) Older children might want to help prepare the dry mix.

Cooking Hints and Safety Tips (please review pages 11–15):

- Use finely gound cornmeal (not the coarser polenta) for best results.
- Use a bowl large enough for enthusiastic mixing.
- Have damp paper towels ready.
- A simple way for young kids to crack an egg is to smack it on the bottom of a pie pan and let the egg run out into the pan. (It's easier to get shells out of the egg than to get egg off the table.) Remind your child to whack the egg really hard.
- Take the stress out of measuring liquids by placing the measuring cup in a pie pan. Let your child pour the buttermilk into the measuring cup. (For a very small child, pour the buttermilk into a small pitcher first.) The pie pan will catch the spills.
- If you have an electric skillet, by all means, use it. This makes the cooking safer because you can put it on a table at a child-accessible level.

- ✦ During the cooking, stay near the pan at all times. Remind younger children that the pan is very hot, and tell them that's why they use the spatula.
- ✦ Cook one pancake at a time for easier flipping.
- ✦ When the pancake is ready to turn, loosen it before your child takes over the flipping. If you are using a gas stove, turn the heat off before flipping, and back on again as soon as you are finished.

Children's Tools: 2 large bowls; pie pan for cracking eggs and catching possible buttermilk spills; 2-cup-capacity liquid measuring cup; dry measuring cups; whisk; long-handled wooden spoon; skillet; 1/2-cup measure with a handle for scooping batter; spatula; a plate and fork for each person

Corny Corn Cakes Recipe

PANCAKE MIX

1/2 cup cornmeal

1/2 cup unbleached all-purpose flour

1/2 teaspoon salt

1 teaspoon baking powder

1/2 teaspoon baking soda

1 tablespoon sugar

2 large eggs

1 cup buttermilk

1 tablespoon butter, melted

1/2 cup corn, fresh or frozen

A little butter for the pan

Syrup, fresh fruit, or powdered sugar for serving

1) To make the Pancake Mix, combine the dry ingredients in a large bowl.
2) Beat the eggs in a separate large bowl, then whisk in the buttermilk, melted butter, and corn.
3) Pour the buttermilk mixture into the dry ingredients. Stir from the bottom of the bowl until the dry ingredients are all moistened.
4) Place a skillet over medium heat, and melt in a little butter. Use a 1/2-cup measure with a handle to scoop batter into the hot skillet.
5) Cook the pancake for about 5 minutes on the first side, or until *really* golden on the bottom. Then flip and cook on the second side, which will go a little faster; usually 2 to 3 minutes will do it, depending on the heat.
6) Serve right away, and eat with syrup, fresh fruit, or powdered sugar.

YIELD: Ten 4-inch pancakes

Corny Corn Cakes

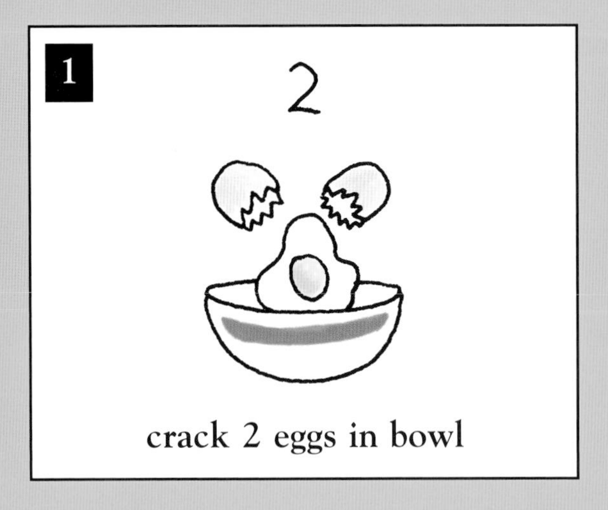

crack 2 eggs in bowl

add 1 cup buttermilk

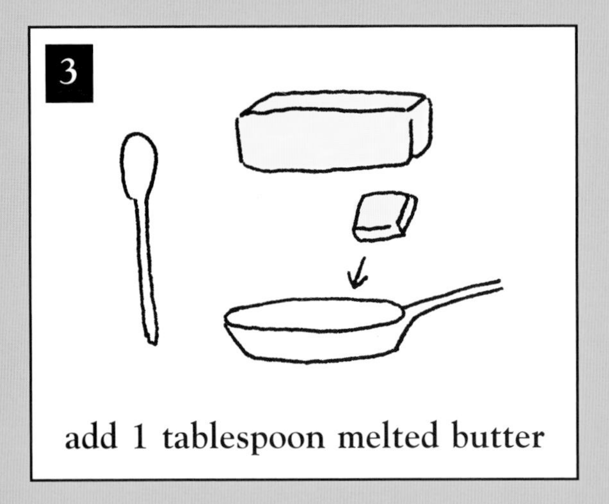

add 1 tablespoon melted butter

add 1/2 cup corn

whisk

pour wet into dry mix

stir

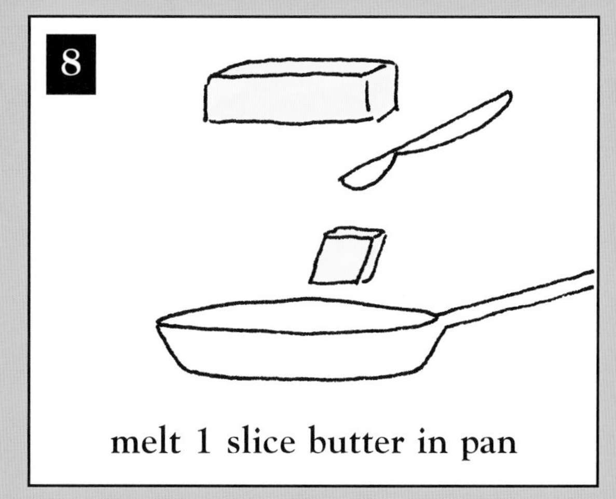

melt 1 slice butter in pan

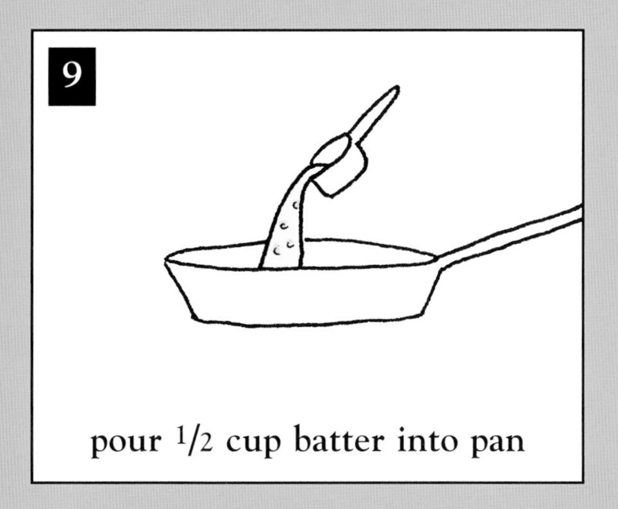

pour 1/2 cup batter into pan

cook

flip and cook

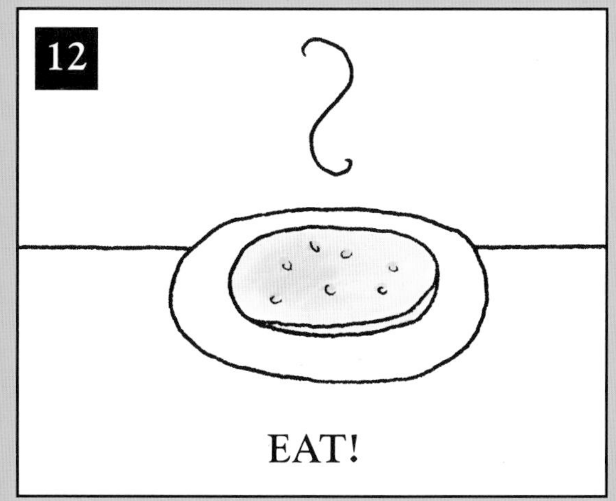

EAT!

The Critics Rave:

When the cheese goes in the pan, it's gonna turn into something. —RACHEL

The cheese is getting crackles. —JULIA

You can hear the ocean from here. —NATE *(placing the blender lid next to his ear)*

I like scooping the soup with my cracker. The soup is like a sauce. —AVRAM

To the Grown-ups:

In this two-part project, the kids first make their own little cheese crackers by melting Parmesan cheese in a skillet and then cooking it on both sides until crisp. This is possibly the most satisfying single-ingredient recipe on the planet! Then, while the crackers cool, the children assemble an ultrasimple tomato soup consisting of canned tomatoes blended with milk. This is a great opportunity to learn that sometimes soup is nothing more than regular food mushed up.

Cooking Hints and Safety Tips (please review pages 11–15):

- ✦ Spraying the skillet with nonstick spray is an adult job, but kids can "help." An adult should hold the can and aim, and a child can press the button. If the spray lands all in one place, just rub it around with a paper towel.
- ✦ The kids spoon the cheese into a cold pan for safety. This way, they can take their time and carefully flatten down the cheese without worry.
- ✦ Before the cheese crackers can be flipped, they must be loosened all around with a spatula. This is an adult job! After loosening the crackers, slide the spatula underneath, and let a child do the flipping and, later, the transferring from the pan to a plate.

- Take the stress out of measuring liquids by placing the measuring cup in a pie pan. Let your child pour the milk into the measuring cup. (For a very small child, pour the milk into a small pitcher first.) The pie pan will catch the spills.
- Kids can push the buttons on the blender. (It's easiest for them to use their thumbs.) With a little adult assistance, they can also pour the soup out of the blender. It must be made very clear that they should never touch the blade.
- Only an adult should handle or serve the heated soup. For safety's sake, just warm the soup, as it does not need to be cooked.

Children's Tools: Skillet; measuring spoons; soupspoons for spreading the cheese; spatula; blender; medium-sized saucepan; 1- or 2-cup-capacity liquid measuring cup; a small plate, bowl, and spoon for each person

Cream of Tomato Soup and Crispy Cheese Crackers Recipe

Nonstick spray for the skillet

1/4 pound Parmesan cheese, grated (1 cup)

1 can (14.5-ounces) crushed tomatoes

1/2 cup milk, at room temperature

1) Lightly spray a skillet with nonstick spray. Place the Parmesan in the pan in little heaps of 1 tablespoon each, and smooth the cheese into thin circles with the back of a spoon.
2) Turn on the heat to medium, and cook the cheese on both sides until it melts and then forms thin, crispy crackers. Remove the crackers from the pan and let them cool on a plate.
3) Place the tomatoes in a blender and purée until smooth. Transfer to a medium-sized saucepan, pour in the milk, and heat until warm.
4) Eat!

YIELD: 2 to 3 servings

Cream of Tomato Soup and Crispy Cheese Crackers

spoon cheese into pan

press cheese down with spoon

cook

flip

cook on the other side

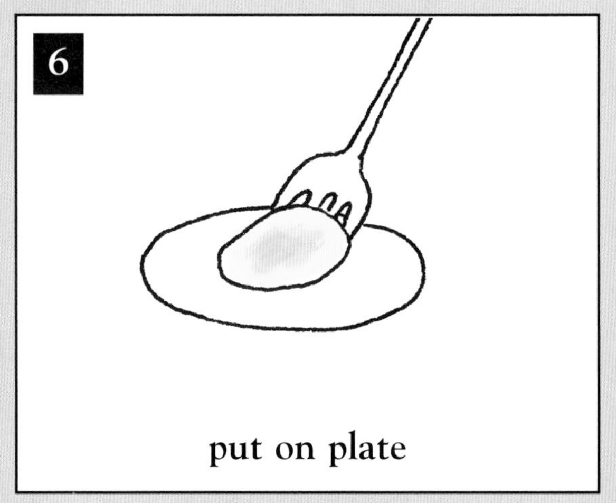

put on plate

put tomatoes in blender

blend

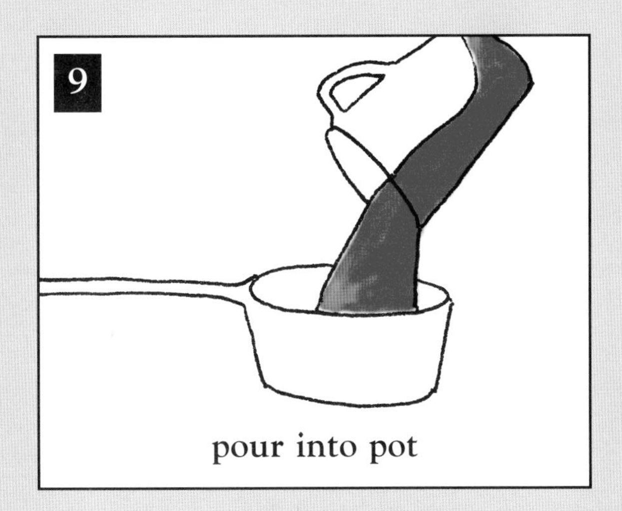

pour into pot

add 1/2 cup milk

heat

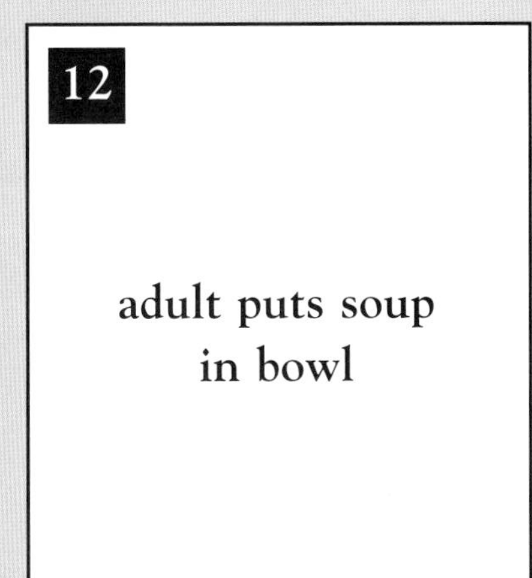

adult puts soup
in bowl

EAT!

The Critics Rave:

This egg doesn't make a sound when I shake it. —MAX

The eggs have a shell so they won't spill. —SARAH

We don't eat the shells, 'cause they'll make our tummy sick. —MIA

They bounce! —LEAH *(observing peeled, unsliced eggs in the bowl)*

This could be lunch. —REBECCA

To the Grown-ups:

The popularity of egg salad among very small children is a delightful surprise! The kids love every aspect of this project and are especially fascinated by the physical properties of hard-boiled eggs, both within and without the shell.

Kids really enjoy peeling eggs. Whack the eggs for them first to loosen the shell. (Or tell them to "Knock it on the table many times, all over the egg," and let them take their time with it.) Rinsing the eggs afterward gets off any remaining shell and is easiest done in a pie pan with tepid water. Have a clean, dry tea towel—or several paper towels—folded into thick layers, and let the children gently roll each rinsed egg on the towel to dry it off before slicing.

Once the mayonnaise is added, the mixing is actually more of a mashing process. The kids can then make sandwiches on bread or crackers, or scoop up the egg salad with sturdy snow peas, cucumber slices, or chunks of celery or red bell pepper.

Cooking Hints and Safety Tips (please review pages 11–15):

- An egg slicer is an ideal child gadget! Tell your child to push the slicing part all the way down slowly, and then to take out the egg before lifting the unit back up. The sliced egg can then be put back on the contraption at a different angle and resliced to make a criss-cross pattern, yielding smaller pieces.
- Use a salt shaker that is neither too fast nor too slow.
- If you want to use this in a sandwich, lightly toast the bread first, so it won't tear when handled exuberantly by your young chef. The easiest way for small children to spread egg salad on toast or crackers is for you spoon it on for them, and then let them mash it down with the back of a spoon.

Children's Tools: Egg slicer; large bowl; measuring cup; salt shaker; long-handled wooden spoon; child-appropriate knives or spoons for spreading; a plate for each person

Egg Salad Recipe

4 large hard-boiled eggs

1/4 cup mayonnaise

6 shakes salt

1) **Peel the eggs thoroughly, rinse them, and put them through an egg slicer, first one way and then again at a 90-degree angle.**
2) **Transfer the egg pieces to a bowl.**
3) **Add the mayonnaise and salt, and mix well.**

YIELD: Enough for 3 to 4 small sandwiches

Egg Salad

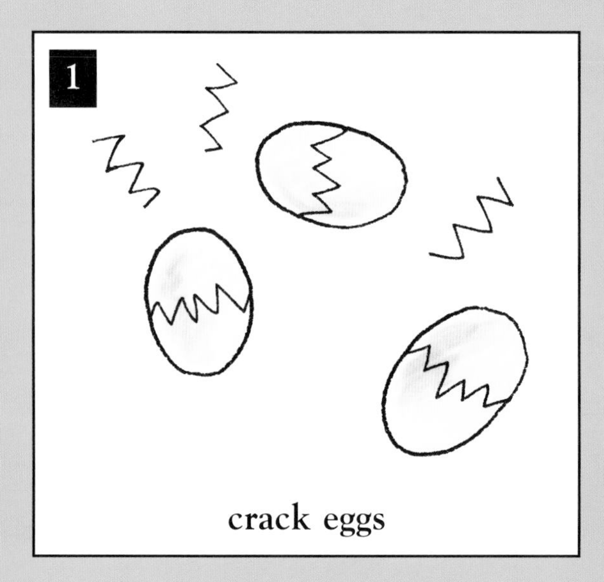

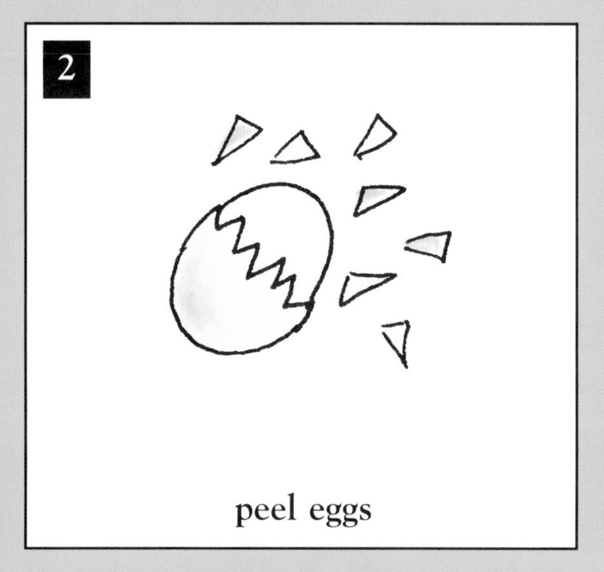

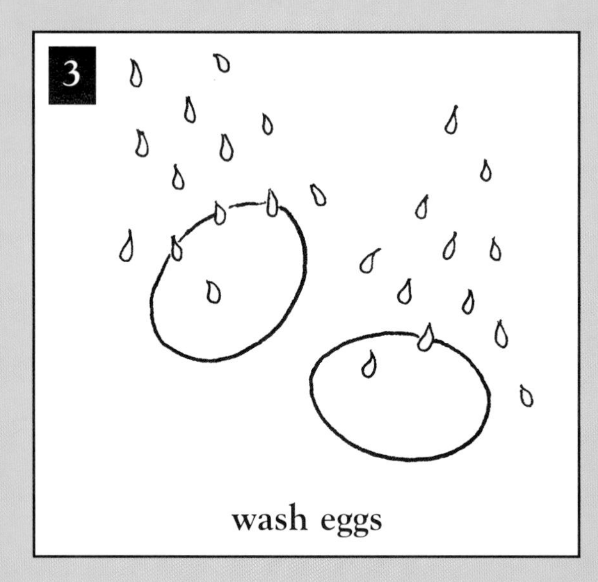

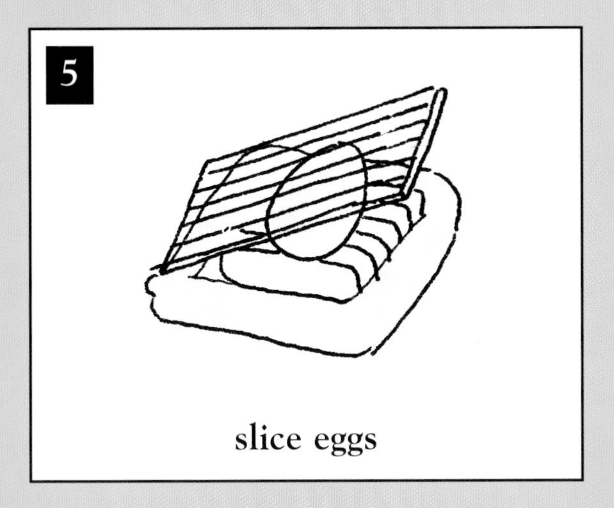

slice eggs

put eggs in bowl

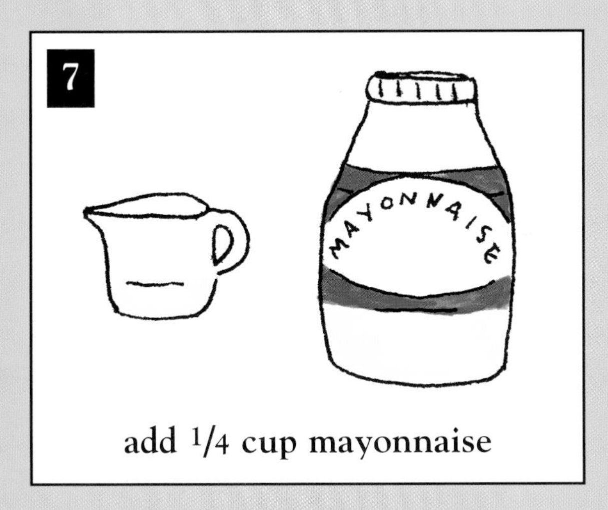

add 1/4 cup mayonnaise

add 6 shakes salt

stir and mash

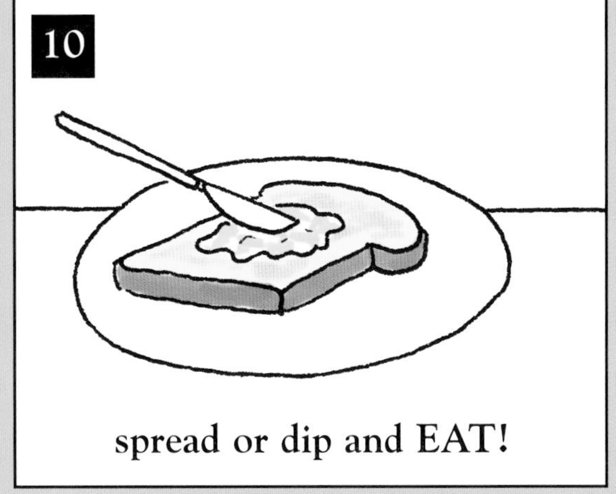

spread or dip and EAT!

The Critics Rave:

Now I have a moustache. —TYLER

I like to snack on the mango pit. —NATE

You can also eat it with a spoon, like soup. —JULIA

To the Grown-ups:

Mango lassi—a purée of buttermilk or yogurt with bright, delicious mango—is a filling and refreshing Indian drink. Buttermilk is especially tangy, and the addition of honey teams up beautifully with the sweet mango to offset the tartness. (It might be interesting for older kids to know that buttermilk originated as the leftover liquid when milk was churned into butter, and that's how it got its name.)

This recipe is designed to make one serving at a time, so be prepared for a repeat performance or two. Once the popularity of this drink becomes established in your household or classroom, you can experiment with adding other soft, ripe fruit in season. Try bananas, strawberries, or peaches—or a combination. You can also use frozen mangoes, which are now available in some grocery stores. No need to defrost them first.

Cooking Hints and Safety Tips (please review pages 11–15):

- ✦ Prepare the mango first by cutting the fruit off the pit and removing the peel. Then your youngsters can have at the mango flesh with child-appropriate knives. Their cutting job is mostly symbolic—it doesn't really matter what size the pieces are, because they will be puréed in the blender.
- ✦ Take the stress out of measuring liquids by placing the measuring cup in a pie pan. Let your child pour the buttermilk into the measuring cup. (For a very small child, pour the buttermilk into a small pitcher first.) The pie pan will catch the spills.
- ✦ Lightly spray the spoon with nonstick spray before measuring the honey. Don't worry too much about the exact measurement.
- ✦ Kids can push the buttons on the blender. (It's easiest for them to use their thumbs.) With a little adult assistance, they can also pour the lassi out of the blender. It must be made very clear that they should never touch the blade.

Children's Tools: Cutting boards and child-appropriate knives; 2-cup-capacity liquid measuring cup; measuring spoons; blender; drinking cup

Mango-Honey Lassi Recipe

1/2 cup chopped mango pulp (about 4 ounces fresh or frozen mango)

3/4 cup buttermilk

Nonstick spray for the honey spoon

1 1/2 teaspoons honey

3 ice cubes

1) Combine the mango, buttermilk, and honey in a blender and blend until smooth.

2) Serve over ice, and drink!

YIELD: 1 serving

Mango-Honey Lassi

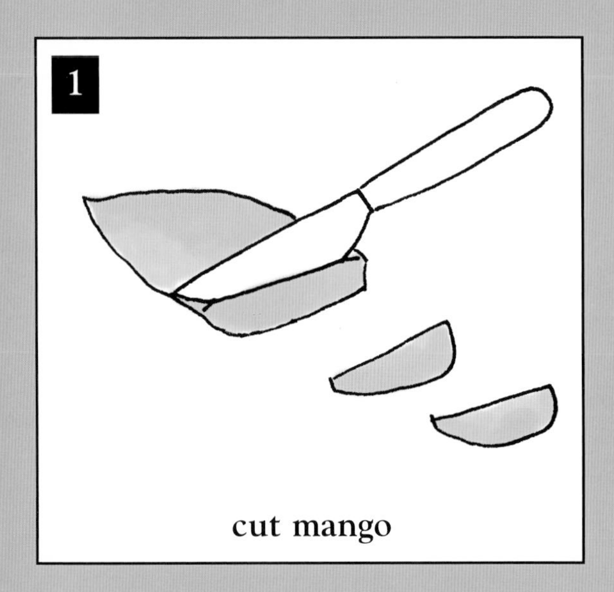

cut mango

put in blender

add 3/4 cup buttermilk

add 1 1/2 teaspoons honey

blend

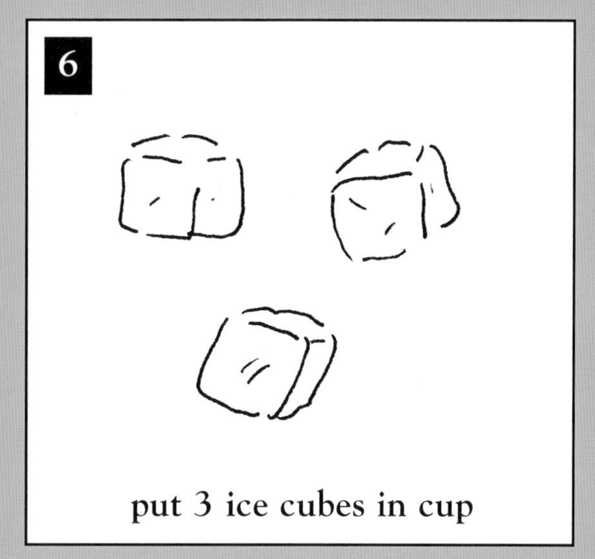

put 3 ice cubes in cup

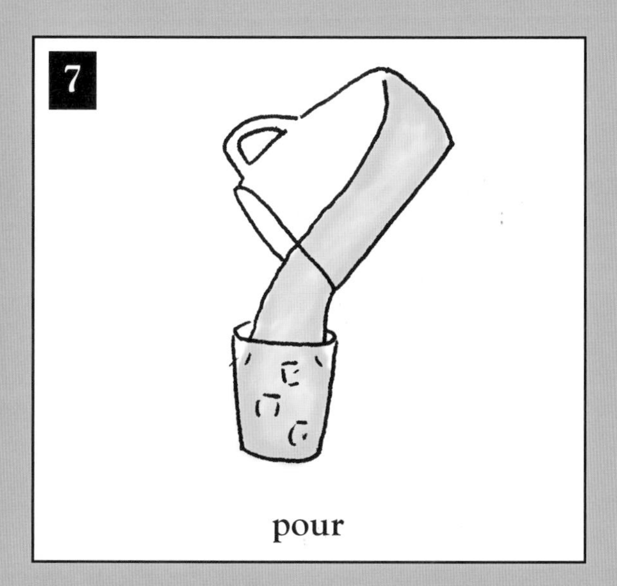

pour

DRINK!

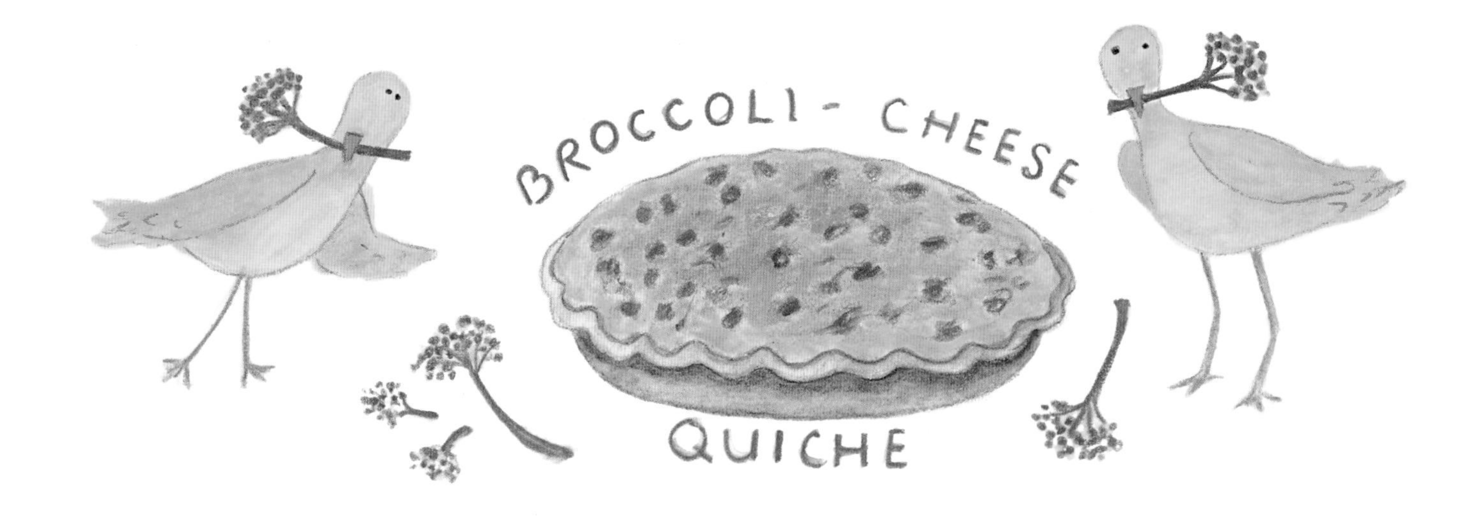

The Critics Rave:

I know what a crust is. It's something you put food in. —JULIA

I broke a egg once before, but it got all over my hands and not in the bowl. —MAX

Does the milk make it taste more good? —ZACHARY

To the Grown-ups:

We normally think of quiche as being very adult. But kids love it too, and it is very easy for them to assemble the filling items once the crust is made. Be sure to let them sniff the scallions—children really appreciate the aromas of seasonings! And the paprika-on-top ritual is especially interesting, as is the transformation of the filling from wet and light yellow to solid and golden during baking. Be prepared for two challenging wait periods—one during baking and the other for cooling. The rewards will be worth it!

Cooking Hints and Safety Tips (please review pages 11–15):

- Raw broccoli can be broken into little pieces by hand. Children can also cut broccoli using child-appropriate knives if it is partially cooked ahead of time.
- Kids may also enjoy helping grate the cheese. Closely supervise the grating, telling your child how it works and warning about the sharp edges. "Be careful of your knuckles!" is an important instruction.
- Use a bowl that is large enough for enthusiastic mixing. You can help by holding it steady. Minimize splashing by beating the eggs well before adding the milk.
- Have damp paper towels ready.

- ✦ A simple way for young kids to crack an egg is to smack it on the bottom of a pie pan and let the egg run out into the pan. (It's easier to get shells out of the egg than to get spilled egg off the table.) Remind your child to whack the egg really hard.
- ✦ Take the stress out of measuring liquids by placing the measuring cup in a pie pan. Let your child pour the milk into the measuring cup. The pie pan will catch the spills.
- ✦ Use a special pitcher (not too heavy) for pouring the egg batter into the crust.
- ✦ Putting the pan into the oven and taking it out are adult jobs!

Children's Tools: Cutting boards and child-appropriate knives (if the children will be cutting); standing grater with large holes (if the children will be grating the cheese); dry measuring cups; extra pie pan for cracking eggs and catching possible milk spills; large bowl; whisk; 2-cup-capacity liquid measuring cup; measuring spoons; pitcher for pouring egg batter into crust; a plate and fork for each person

Broccoli-Cheese Quiche Recipe

1 1/2 cups chopped broccoli

1 cup (packed) grated Swiss cheese

1 unbaked 9-inch pie shell (storebought or homemade)—not deep-dish

4 large eggs

2/3 cup milk

1/4 teaspoon salt

2 scallions, trimmed of roots and finely minced (white and green parts)

4 shakes paprika

1) Preheat the oven to 350°F.
2) Steam the broccoli over simmering water until bright green and just tender. Refresh in a strainer under cold running water, then drain and dry thoroughly.
3) Sprinkle the cheese into the crust, then distribute the broccoli over the cheese. In a large bowl, whisk the eggs until smooth. Add the milk, salt, and scallions, and whisk until blended. Pour this mixture over the broccoli and cheese.
4) Dust the top with paprika, and bake in the center of the oven for 40 minutes, or until solid in the center when gently shaken. Cool on a rack for at least 15 minutes (it can be served warm or at room temperature), then eat!

YIELD: 4 to 6 servings (1 small pie)

Broccoli-Cheese Quiche

put cheese in crust

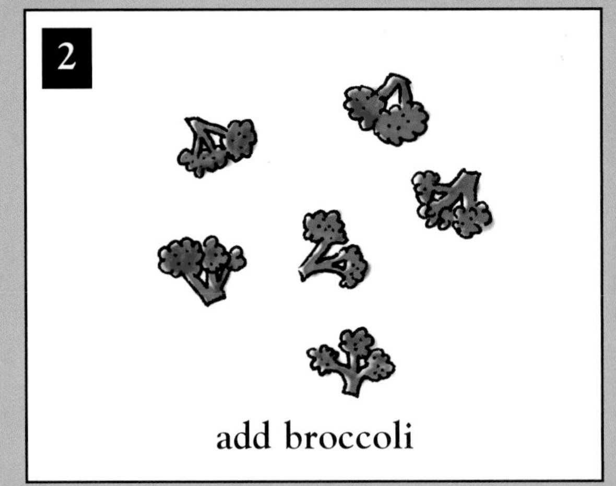

add broccoli

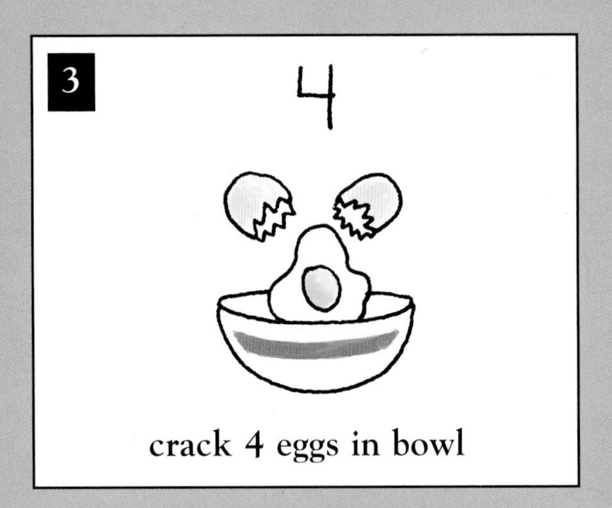

crack 4 eggs in bowl

whisk eggs

add 2/3 cup milk

add 1/4 teaspoon salt

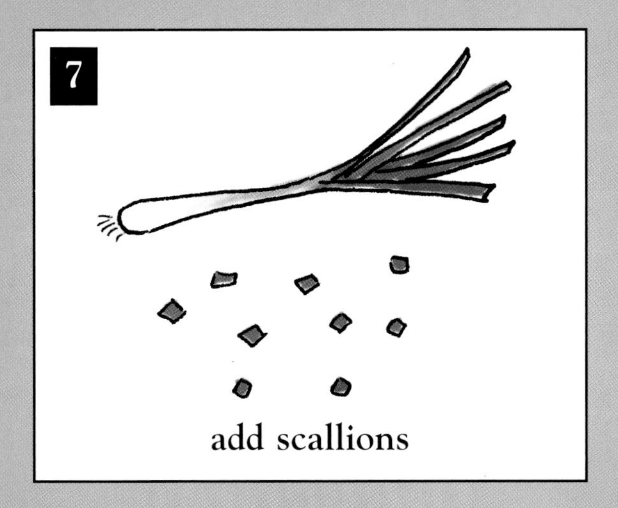

add scallions

whisk slowly

pour into crust

sprinkle 4 shakes paprika

bake 40 minutes

EAT!

The Critics Rave:

These are children-size! —JULIA

It looks like little pancakes. Where's the syrup? —RAYMOND

Accidentally you sprayed my arm. —MARTIN

I want another one, please. —DAVID

To the Grown-ups:

An alternative to expensive and often nutritionally overrated energy bars, these little circles are made from oats, soy protein powder (available in bulk bins in most natural food stores; substitute flour if you can't find it), and other good-for-you ingredients. Children especially appreciate the diminutive result—truly to scale. The ingredients are very pleasantly tactile, so if you make it in a big bowl, the kids can roll up their sleeves and mix it directly with their clean hands. The batter is forgiving and doesn't mind a lot of handling, although kids will need help with mixing and putting the batter into the muffin cups. They can pat the batter down themselves (and they like to take their time with it).

To simplify this recipe, first make a mix of the basic dry ingredients to which your child can then add the oats, sugar, cinnamon, raisins, and wet ingredients. Older children might want to help prepare the mix.

Cooking Hints and Safety Tips (please review pages 11–15):

- ✦ Ultraclean hands today! Keep damp paper towels handy.
- ✦ Spraying the muffin cups with nonstick spray is an adult job, but kids can "help." An adult should hold the can and aim, and a child can press the button. If the spray lands all in one place, just rub it around with a paper towel.
- ✦ Take the stress out of measuring liquids by placing the measuring cup in a pie pan. Let your child pour or spoon the yogurt and oil into the measuring cup. The pie pan will catch the spills.
- ✦ The batter is quite sticky. This is fine for (literally) hand-mixing, but when it comes time to pat the batter into the muffin cups, the kids will need to flour their hands ("wash hands with flour") or have their palms and fingers covered with a light coating of nonstick spray.
- ✦ Putting the pans into the oven and taking them out—and then removing the Energy Circles from the pan—are adult jobs! Let the Energy Circles cool down before serving.

Children's Tools: Standard muffin pans; large bowl; dry measuring cups; measuring spoons; 2-cup-capacity liquid measuring cup; small whisk; long-handled wooden spoon; rubber spatula

Chewy Energy Circles Recipe

Nonstick spray for the pan

DRY MIX

1 cup unbleached all-purpose flour

3/4 cup soy protein powder

1/2 teaspoon salt

2 cups rolled oats

1/2 teaspoon cinnamon

2/3 cup brown sugar

1/2 cup raisins

1 1/2 cups vanilla yogurt

1/4 cup canola oil

1) Preheat the oven to 375°F. Spray 24 standard-size muffin cups with nonstick spray.
2) Combine the flour, protein powder, and salt in a large bowl.
3) Add the oats, cinnamon, brown sugar, and raisins and mix with clean hands.
4) Measure the yogurt into a 2-cup measure. Add the oil and use a fork or small whisk to combine them directly in the cup.
5) Add wet to dry, and mix with hands until completely combined.
6) Place approximately 1 1/2 tablespoons of the batter in each muffin cup and pat or poke into place.
7) Bake in the center of the oven for 12 to 15 minutes, or until brown around the edges. Transfer to a rack and cool for at least 10 minutes, then eat!

YIELD: About 24 small circles

Chewy Energy Circles

put 2 cups oats in bowl

add 1/2 teaspoon cinnamon

add 2/3 cup brown sugar

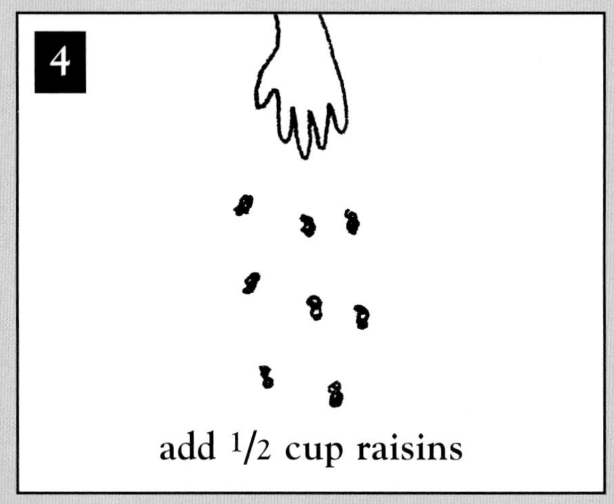

add 1/2 cup raisins

mix with hands

put 1 1/2 cups vanilla yogurt
in cup

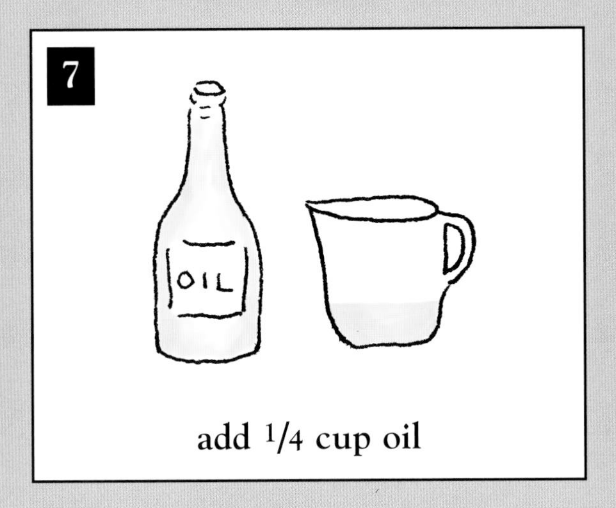

7

add 1/4 cup oil

8

whisk the wet

9

pour wet into dry

10

mix

11

put into muffin cups

12

bake 15 minutes

13

EAT!

The Critics Rave:

If you squish a chickpea, it will look like a butterfly. —MIA

If we stir it fast, it will come out of the pot. —GABRIELLE

Wow! What a soup! —NATE

To the Grown-ups:

The first step of this recipe has the children making a classic basil pesto, which is a tremendously popular item among preschoolers. This time, though, instead of dumping the pesto onto cooked pasta (as the kids do for Green Spaghetti in *Pretend Soup*), the young chefs spoon it into a very adult, very Italian soup containing chickpeas and macaroni. The pesto becomes the soup's topping—and ultimately its seasoning—and the kids love mixing it in and watching the subtle color changes as they do.

To make this project safe, the children fill their bowls with the chickpeas and macaroni, and then the adult adds the broth. The kids finish it off with a spoonful of pesto. An easy assembly job!

Cooking Hints and Safety Tips (please review pages 11–15):

- Make sure the macaroni, chickpeas, and pesto are at room temperature before beginning the project, so they won't cool down the broth too much.
- Children love removing basil leaves from the stems, but they might need to be reminded to save the former and discard the latter.
- An effective and satisfying way to remove garlic skin is to put the clove on a cutting board and let your child smash it with a can of soup.

- It works best if your child holds the empty measuring cup over the food processor and you pour the oil into the cup. When the cup is full, your child can dump the oil into the processor.
- Kids can push the buttons on the processor. (It's easiest for them to use their thumbs.) They can also scrape out the pesto with a rubber spatula once the blade has been removed. It must be made very clear that they should never touch the blade.
- Use a salt shaker that is neither too fast nor too slow.
- Only an adult should handle or serve the hot broth. For safety's sake, *warm* the broth, rather than heating it to a very high temperature. It does not need to be cooked.

Children's Tools: Food processor; can of soup (for smashing garlic); dry measuring cups; 1-cup-capacity liquid measuring cup; salt shaker; rubber spatula; a bowl and spoon for each person

Pesto-Macaroni Soup Recipe

3 packed cups basil leaves
1 medium clove garlic
1/4 cup grated Parmesan cheese
1/4 cup extra virgin olive oil
6 shakes salt
2 cups cooked macaroni
1 can (15-ounces) chickpeas, drained and rinsed
4 cups vegetable broth, heated

1) Take the basil leaves off the stems. Discard the stems, and put the leaves into the food processor.
2) Smash and peel the garlic. Add it to the basil, and blend until uniform.
3) Add the cheese, oil, and salt, and blend again until it forms a thick paste. Transfer to a bowl.
4) Place the macaroni and chickpeas in separate bowls.
5) Spoon macaroni and chickpeas into individual serving bowls, then ladle warm broth over the top.
6) Add a spoonful of pesto to each serving, and stir it in.
7) Eat!

NOTE: There are some very good varieties of vegetable broth available in supermarkets. I prefer Imagine brand, which comes unrefrigerated in a 1-quart box (like soymilk).

YIELD: 5 to 6 servings

Pesto-Macaroni Soup

take off basil leaves

smash and peel garlic

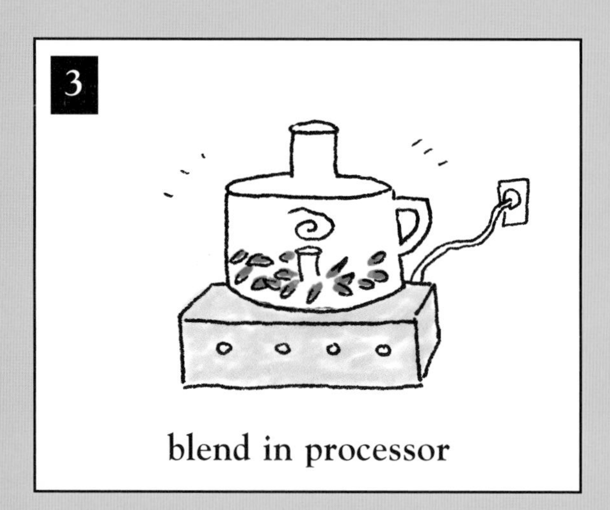

blend in processor

add 1/4 cup cheese

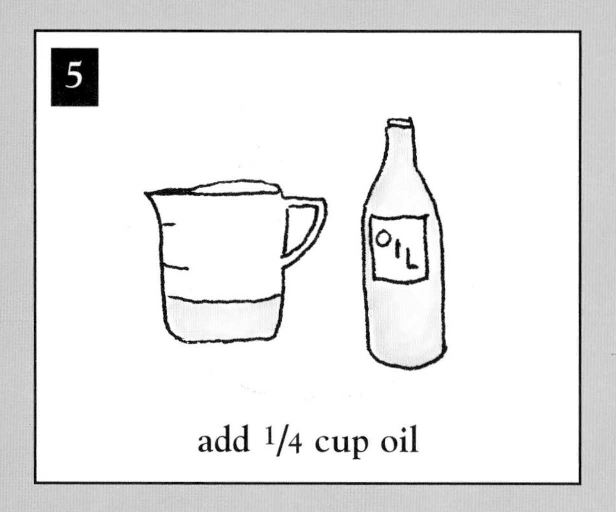

add 1/4 cup oil

add 6 shakes salt

blend again

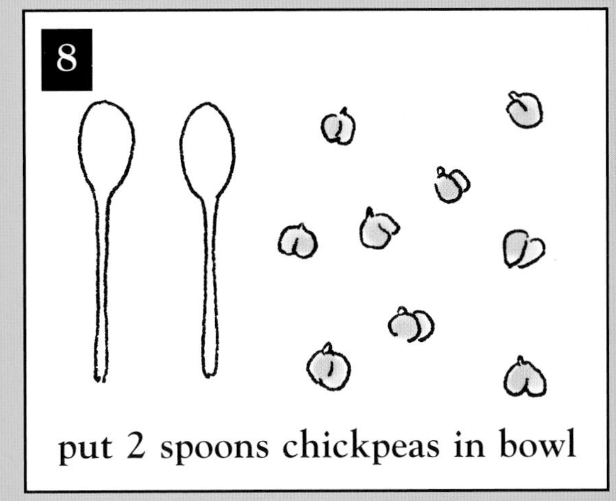

put 2 spoons chickpeas in bowl

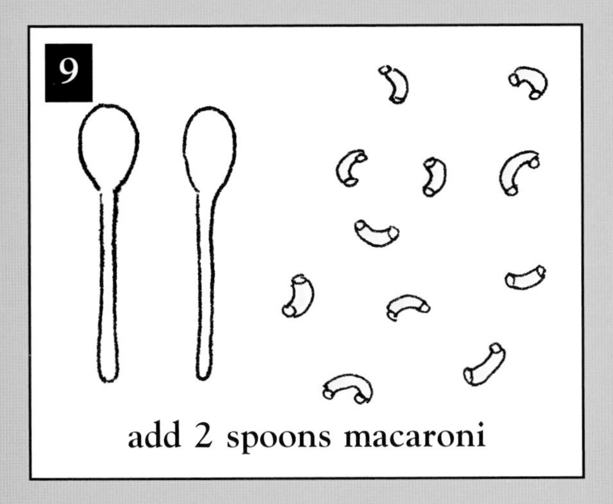

add 2 spoons macaroni

10

adult adds broth

add 1 spoon pesto

stir and EAT!

The Critics Rave:

That's a lot of raspberries! —REBECCA

We can't count the seeds because there's too many! —MARTIN

Now it's sauce! —ZACHARY

Smell it! It's gonna be delicious! —KATE

To the Grown-ups:

In this cheerful project, the kids make a bright red raspberry purée and then swirl it onto a plateful of vanilla yogurt. A delicious snack is the result, satisfying everyone's sweet tooth *and* appetite. Even though the berries are measured, children like to count them as they put them in the blender. And they *love* to strain the sauce! Give this part a lot of time, reminding the young chefs to keep the stirring slow and low-key.

Cooking Hints and Safety Tips (please review pages 11–15):

- ✦ Kids can push the buttons on the blender. (It's easiest for them to use their thumbs.) With a little adult assistance, they can also pour the sauce out of the blender. It must be made very clear that they should never touch the blade.
- ✦ Don't use too fine a strainer, or the purée will get stuck and just sit there. You want it to be able to stop raspberry seeds while letting purée drip through.
- ✦ Use a funnel to transfer the sauce to a squeeze bottle.

✦ When squeezing out the raspberry sauce, help the child move the bottle around while squirting, so it doesn't land in one big pile. Although it might take several tries to get a design going, this recipe is so popular that the kids will likely want seconds.

Children's Tools: Blender; measuring spoons; strainer; bowl that fits the strainer; rubber spatula; funnel; plastic squeeze bottle; 1- or 2-cup-capacity liquid measuring cup; a plate, toothpick, and spoon for each person

Raspberry-Yogurt Swirl Recipe

1 1/2 cups raspberries (fresh or frozen unsweetened)

2 tablespoons sugar

3 tablespoons apple juice concentrate, defrosted

2 cups vanilla yogurt

1) Put the raspberries in a blender with the sugar and apple juice concentrate.
2) Purée.
3) Place a strainer over a bowl, and pour the purée into the strainer. Stir until the purée passes into the bowl and only the seeds are left in the strainer.
4) Funnel the raspberry purée into a plastic squeeze bottle and tightly screw on the lid.
5) For each serving, place 1/2 cup yogurt on a plate and spread it into a circle about 5 inches across.
6) Squeeze raspberry purée onto the yogurt in any chosen design, and if desired, swirl it with a toothpick.
7) Eat with a spoon!

NOTE: If you use frozen unsweetened raspberries for this, you will need to defrost them at least halfway. Save and include the juices that the berries emit as they defrost.

Raspberry-Yogurt Swirl

put raspberries in blender

add 2 tablespoons sugar

add 3 tablespoons
apple juice concentrate

blend

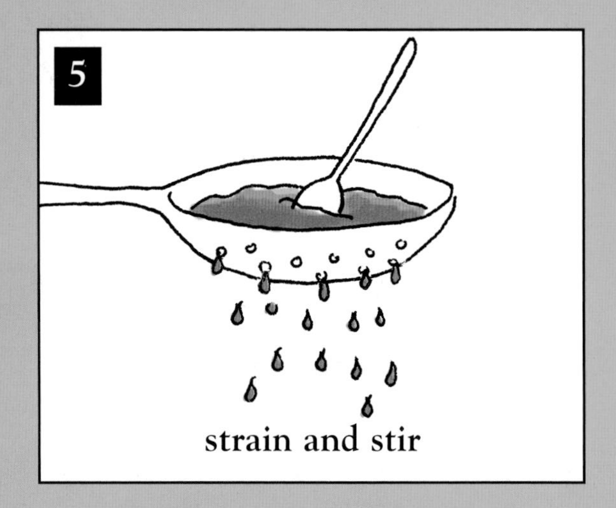

strain and stir

pour into bottle
through funnel

put top on bottle

put 1/2 cup yogurt on plate

spread yogurt with spoon

squirt raspberries

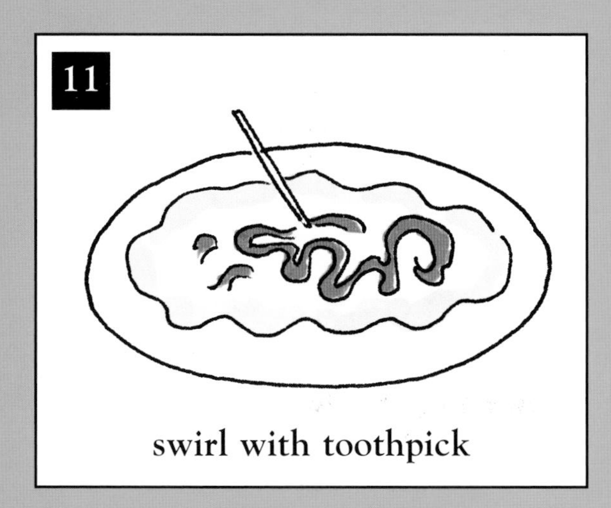

swirl with toothpick

EAT!

Mollie Katzen's cookbooks have sold over 5 million copies!

The New Moosewood Cookbook

Since its original publication in 1977, this influential and enormously popular cookbook has been at the forefront of the revolution in American eating habits.

8½ x 11 inches, 256 pages, 16-page color insert
paper ISBN 1-58008-130-4
hardcover ISBN 1-58008-135-5

The New Enchanted Broccoli Forest

This second volume in Mollie Katzen's classic cooking series features more than 200 vegetarian recipes and a bounty of kitchen guidance from one of America's dearest cookbook authors.

8½ x 11 inches, 320 pages, 16-page color insert
paper ISBN 1-58008-126-6
hardcover ISBN 1-58008-136-3

Still Life with Menu Cookbook

REVISED

Revised to accommodate over 200 low-fat and easy-to-follow recipes, this gorgeously illustrated cookbook presents complete vegetarian menus that range from simple and comforting to absolutely elegant.

8½ x 11 inches, 256 pages, full color
paper ISBN 0-89815-669-6

Pretend Soup and Other Real Recipes

A COOKBOOK FOR PRESCHOOLERS & UP

This delightful, award-winning "first cookbook" for young children features 19 illustrated vegetarian recipes. A great resource for teaching children to cook healthful, appealing food. *Horn Book* calls it "an unusually accessible, attractive, process-oriented cookbook for pre-schoolers...with imaginative and appealing recipes."

8 x 10 inches, 96 pages, full color
hardcover ISBN 1-883672-06-6

Honest Pretzels

AND 64 OTHER AMAZING RECIPES FOR KIDS AGES 8 & UP

For kids who are ready to help with dinner for real. Lively watercolors brighten 60 kid-tested recipes "that work for children.... *Honest Pretzels* is a winner.... It engages the senses, teaches basic skills, and makes for plenty of good eating." —*Riverbank Review*

ALA NOTABLE CHILDREN'S BOOK
CBC CHILDREN'S CHOICE

8 x 10 inches, 192 pages, full color
hardcover ISBN 1-883672-88-0

Available at your local bookstore or from the publisher

P.O. Box 7123 • Berkeley, California 94707
800-841-BOOK • www.tenspeed.com